2013

THE SPORTSMAN'S AUTHORITY S

D0899653

Trophy Whitetails

WALK THE DEER TRAIL WITH *Outdoor Life's* TOP BIG-BUCK EXPERTS

CREATIVE
PUBLISHING
international

MINNETONKA, MINNESOTA

Creative Publishing international, Inc.
5900 Green Oak Drive
Minnetonka, MN 55343
1-800-328-3895

CREATIVE
PUBLISHING
international

Chairman: Iain Macfarlane
President/CEO: David D. Murphy
Vice President/Retail Sales & Marketing: James Knapp
Creative Director: Lisa Rosenthal

TROPHY WHITETAILS
Executive Editor, Outdoor Group: Don Oster
Project Leader and Article Editor : David L. Tieszen
Managing Editor: Jill Anderson
Associate Creative Director: Brad Springer
Photo Researcher: Angie Hartwell
Copy Editor: Janice Cauley
Mac Designer: Joe Fahey
Production Services Manager: Kim Gerber

Contributing Photographers: Charles J. Alsheimer, Erwin A. Bauer, Gary Clancy,
Byron W. Dalrymple, Charles Elliott, Michael H. Francis, Donald M. Jones,
Bill Kinney, Lance Krueger, Bill Marchel, Bill McRae, Jack O'Connor, David
Sams/Texas Inprint, Mark E. Scott, Jim Zumbo

Contributing Illustrators: Tom Beecham, John Dyess, Ken Laager, Charles E. Pearson,
Jeffrey Terreson

Cover Illustrator: Leon Parson

Printed on American paper by: R. R. Donnelley & Sons Co.

10 9 8 7 6 5 4 3 2 1

Library of Congress Cataloging-in-Publication Data

Trophy whitetails : walk the deer trail with Outdoor life's top big
  -buck experts.
       p.   cm.
    At head of title: Outdoor life.
    ISBN 0-86573-104-7 (softcover)
    1. White-tailed deer hunting.   I. Creative Publishing
International.   II.   Title: Outdoor life
SK301.T73   1999
779.2'7652--dc21   99-33020

Table of Contents

Introduction

Whitetail deer hunting books are unquestionably the most popular among all the big-game hunting books published. No surprise there, since whitetails are by far the most sought–after deer in the country.

So why do we need another whitetail book, and why should you read this one? Good question, and one with an answer.

Hunting books offer two kinds of reading – the educational book that describes how to make you a more savvy hunter with lots of tips and techniques, and the entertainment book that is best enjoyed in your favorite chair, allowing you to experience hunts vicariously through the eyes of the authors.

Trophy Whitetails presents both. In these pages you'll learn all sorts of tricks and strategies by knowledgeable hunter/authors such as Gary Clancy, Michael Hanback, Michael Pearce, Charles J. Alsheimer and others. These writers don't dream up stuff – they're out in the trenches of the whitetail woods, gleaning information that eventually is passed on to readers like you. You'll learn the latest on scrapes, scents, rubs, when to hunt, stands, drives, stillhunting, shooting and all sorts of other gems of wisdom.

The easy-reading part of the book brings you classic stories penned by writers who are no strangers to hunters, like the late Jack O'Connor, the legendary former Shooting Editor of *Outdoor Life*, who wrote hundreds of thrilling articles for the magazine. And Charles Elliott, *Outdoor Life's* Southern Editor, who, at 94 and still writing strong, has hundreds of big-game hunting trips under his belt, including 32 straight elk hunts in the Wyoming wilderness. And Erwin Bauer, known simply as "Joe" by his peers, who has written countless articles for outdoor magazines.

Chances are good you won't put *Trophy Whitetails* down once you begin reading it, which makes a good book a great book. This is a great book.

Jim Zumbo, Hunting Editor, Outdoor Life

The Hunt

The Phases of Fall

by Michael Pearce

Seasonal changes and hormones bind whitetails to a time clock. Learn a buck's schedule and you can find him.

FIFTY-ONE WEEKS OF ANTICIPATION made this sunrise seem like the longest in history. Since being here a year ago, the stand in the gnarled old Missouri oak tree had settled into my memory like an old friend. The previous season it had served up an unforgettable morning. In barely an hour, six whitetail bucks had passed below its limbs within bow range.

Some had moved through at a steady trot, noses to the ground as they searched for passing does. Others had already found potential mates and had burst onto the timbered flat, chasing and herding does like shepherd dogs.

The biggest of the bunch, a record-class eight-pointer with chocolate-colored horns, had been the icing on the cake. He'd walked stiff-legged toward the sound of my grunt call with his hair on end. It was a shot that even I couldn't miss.

Now, back in the stand, I knew I couldn't expect a repeat performance, but my confidence was high as I waited for daylight. A check the previous afternoon had shown acorns again falling on the high Ozark ridge, and deer tracks pocked the soft mud beside the pond below the stand. Though not as impressive as the year before, rubs and scrapes dotted the old two-track road that crossed the area.

By the end of my second day it was obvious that the area was missing one crucial ingredient—whitetail bucks. Does were common enough, grazing on the acorns and other mast, stopping at the pond and moving in and out of the brushy bedding areas that ringed the ridge. But after spending more than 15 hours in the stand I saw only one scrawny buck. The scrapes were being hit only sporadically at night.

I climbed down from the stand that second evening, feeling more educated than disappointed. With the number of does around, the flat could eventually be the best place on the farm to arrow a nice whitetail buck. But not for the time being.

That night back at the cabin a conversation confirmed my plans for changing stands.

"With all the food, water and bedding area for does, that place will probably be swarming with bucks later on," said Brad Harris, a product designer for Lohman Game Calls who routinely spends 100 days a year videotaping, scouting and hunting whitetails. "But it'll probably be during the peak of rut. We're hunting a week earlier this year, and they haven't reached that phase yet."

The phase he'd referred to was one of the behavioral periods that whitetails transcend every year. Understanding these phases is one of the most important concepts of deer hunting.

"There is no one best place to take a buck throughout the fall," Harris said. "Whitetails, particularly bucks, can go through up to six different phases during the hunting seasons. A stand that's over-run with bucks during one phase may be nearly devoid of them during others."

These phases are easy to learn, recognize and follow. Though schedules vary across the nation (patterns in northern states may develop as much as two months before similar activity in deep Dixie), the sequence is basically the same anywhere whitetails roam.

Bachelor Days

Late in the summer, before most seasons open, bucks are often in herds, feeding in secluded fields just before dark. During the lazy, hot days the deer are less skittish. It's a great time to see the quality of the bucks that will be using an area later on.

As they begin to lose their velvet, the bucks will part company and become more secretive. Many, particularly the older ones, will become nocturnal feeders and daytime sleepers. Your best chance for success will usually come between these two daily patterns.

I used this tactic on an Alabama hunt after discovering that the bucks were still in the bachelor phase. Although the rut was over in my native Kansas, it was still weeks away down South. After a morning of watching does and fawns from the stands placed in various patches of hardwoods, my host decided I needed to try another setup.

"The bucks aren't even really into scrapes or rubs and they're not hanging around the does yet," said Dave Lyon, co-owner of Southern Sportsmen's Lodge near Haneyville. "They're feeding at night and spending their days back in the swamps. That's where you'll be in the morning."

Well before dawn I followed Lyon's trail markers to a ladder stand in a moss-covered cypress tree. He had told me that the deer would be sneaking back into the thick swamp in front of me after feeding all night.

Less than an hour into the next day I glimpsed a pair of bucks easing through the palmettos. A roundball from my Hatfield muzzleloader dropped one of the matching eight-pointers when he slowed to cross a small creek.

Pre-Rut

The pre-rut phase is probably your best chance at patterning a particular buck. It's the week or two prior to peak breeding when whitetail bucks start feeling the urge. It's a time of increased activity as the deer make and check scrapes.

"You can tell the pre-rut stage is starting when you begin seeing more deer moving during the day and you start seeing some rubs and scrapes on main deer trails," said Harris. "Early on you'll find a few scrapes that aren't being heavily used. Bucks will become more and more active as the rut draws near. Hunting over scrapes can be deadly when the pre-rut phase is running strong. Calling, especially rattling and grunting, can also be very, very deadly."

The trick, however, is knowing which scrapes to watch. A scrape or series of scrapes may not be visited by a buck for a week or more. On the other hand, Harris says that he has seen seven different bucks check the same scrape in a single day.

Bigger bucks often prefer scrapes near thick cover and often come no closer than 20 yards downwind from the area to sniff for willing does. Hunter watching a single scrape should set up 25 to 30 yards downwind. Or, if you're on a scrape line, set up where you can cover several scrapes.

Once you've set up in your stand, don't make the mistake of leaving a good scrape too early in the day.

"If they're wound up, you're almost as likely to see a buck using a scrape at noon as you are at first light," said Harris.

Rut

It's usually not hard to tell when the peak of the rut arrives, and it occurs about the same time year after year. For most avid trophy hunters it's a date that's as easily recalled as a birthday.

A simple drive around your hunting area will usually reveal if the whitetails are rutting. Bucks you didn't know existed may be standing in a stupor at the side of the road, wondering where to look next for a hot doe. Lonely fawns are another good indication. Bucks that are chasing does often separate the females from their fawns.

Most big bucks don't follow a pattern during peak rut. That means that you don't need a Ph.D. in wildlife biology to know where to set up during this wildest phase of the fall. The Missouri timbered flat I hunted from the old oak tree with the pond, falling acorns and abundance of bedding cover was a perfect big-woods rut hunting area. The habitat attracted females, and the concentration of does brought bucks running, smelly and stiff-legged with thoughts of propagating the species. No matter where you hunt during the rut, if you find does you'll find bucks.

Don't forget your calls. Rattling and snorts can be irresistible to rutting bucks. Bleat calls can also attract does that have been separated from their fawns. Bucks trailing or chasing those does will sure follow.

Post-Rut

The rut can end as quickly as it begins. A doe-filled alfalfa field can be crawling with bucks one weekend and back to nothing but females and fawns the next.

Post-rut bucks spend much of their time feeding and resting, recuperating from the strenuous ordeal. Because they are not moving as much, the hunting can be difficult—deer drives are probably the best method. Unless you've pinpointed a buck, standhunting can be tough now that the whitetails are not following any solid patterns.

Sometimes it pays to watch the doe areas, hoping to find a buck that's lingering in the rut. Or try setting up between feeding and bedding areas. Hunt early and late in the day when deer are most likely to move.

Secondary Rut

Most parts of America will again see bug-eyed bucks looking for does late in the year.

"You can usually count on our bucks having a second fling in early December," says Charles Alsheimer, a respected whitetail photographer, author and hunting expert from Bath, New York. "It's a time for hunting around the good food sources. I know that if I can find does, bucks in the area are going to come looking."

Much of the secondary rut activity revolves around yearling does, which usually come into estrus a month or two after mature does. Alsheimer says that he's seen rutting activity around young does as late as January, but this phase can linger even later in more southerly regions.

Survival

With more states offering late blackpowder and bowhunts, deer hunters are finding themselves facing a phase that can offer the easiest or the hardest hunting of the year. The end of the secondary rut and the onslaught of winter push bucks into a phase of simple survival. Weakened and thinned from weeks of heavy activity, they know they need to build their strength fast.

Their main concerns are food and warmth. Hunters who find the right combination can do extremely well. When the weather is warm and food is abundant, the hunting can be tough. But if the weather is bad and the deer are concentrated around a single crop field, patch of mast or browse near heavy cover, you could see several good bucks a day. Now is when deer stay close to a secure food source for extended periods of time. Look for standing crops, areas with good mast production or sun-facing slopes where food and warmth are most accessible. If pine thickets or other wind-blocking cover is nearby, all the better.

The deer, which are trying to reserve energy, will travel sparingly this time of year and will remain near a good habitat. So if you find an area with tracks and other signs, there's a good chance deer are nearby.

Pick a Pattern

No matter what phase of the fall, if you spot a pattern, waste no time taking advantage of it. The sooner you set up, the better your chances for success.

It was just such a move that led me from famine to feast on my last year's Missouri bowhunt. Realizing the bucks weren't rutting, I abandoned the stand in the old oak tree. The next morning my hunting partner, Ray Sanderson, and I started checking scrapes for aggressive pre-rut activity.

Most scrapes were small and unexciting. But our faces lit up when we came to where an old two-track road met a clear-cut. Sanderson had found a single scrape in this spot a few days earlier, now there were five! Three were the size of washtubs and had the look and smell of fresh and constant tending. We slipped a tree stand into a nearby red oak.

I climbed into the tree the next morning and hung a pack full of supplies on a limb as I prepared for an all-day vigil. But the pack wasn't needed—I was back in camp for breakfast.

Shortly after shooting light arrived, a fine eight-pointer with a rack studded with pinkie-size sticker points began working the scrapes. I watched him for a half-hour, both fascinated and frustrated. Time after time I'd begin to draw but for a variety of reasons couldn't get a shot. Then, just as he was about to walk into a shooting lane, a breeze gave him my scent and he was gone.

A few minutes later a small spike buck skirted the area, obviously nervous about being caught on a bigger buck's territory. When he spooked and headed west I looked to the east and saw the reason. A buck that appeared to be an eight-pointer was thrashing the farthest scrape.

Having learned my lesson on the previous buck, I blew a few grunts to speed the buck's progress. The first note brought the buck's head to attention and the second pulled him right in.

As the buck neared, I could see that his rack was missing brow tines and that his left antler was chipped. Then, not eight yards from where I sat, I watched him display the move that probably led to his tarnished crown. Rearing up, he raked the branch over the nearest scrape with his rack and rubbed it with his face. I drew my bow while he was churning fresh earth with his hoofs and released my arrow when he finally paused. He was down in seconds.

Anticipation is again building for this year's Missouri hunt. Where will I hunt—a patch of oaks, a scrape line or maybe near a bedding area?

Who knows? I'll have to wait and let the bucks decide for me. Where I'll succeed depends on their phase of the fall. ◆

From Outdoor Life, *September 1994*

Get Your Buck on Opening Day

by Gerald Almy

Strategies for making the best of the first hours of the season.

◆

I F YOU WANT TO KILL A WHITETAIL buck this year, be sure you hunt on the first day of the season. If you don't you may be passing up your best chance to bring in the venison.

Most big-game hunters know that opening day offers rich potential for killing a buck, but many would be surprised to find out just how fruitful this first day is—and how bleak prospects are for scoring during the rest of the season in comparison.

Figures compiled by state fish and wildlife agencies show that the first-day kill of bucks often adds up to from 33 percent to 80 percent of the harvest for the entire season. In Pennsylvania, for example, one of the nation's premier whitetail states, two-thirds of all bucks taken during the 12-day season are dropped on the opener. That means twice as many deer are killed in Pennsylvania on the first day of hunting as during the entire remaining 11 days of the season.

While opening day is not as important in states that have longer seasons, it is for the vast majority of hunters the high-odds time to take a deer.

I always had considered opening day to be important, but its full significance really began to strike home on the first day of West Virginia's deer season several years ago. Dawn came slowly to the wooded hollow where I sat perched on a rough-hewn lumber tree stand. Almost immediately after dawn, I saw a doe and two fawns come ambling down from a nearby field. They paused near my stand, and the doe looked back.

That was the giveaway. Far in the distance a buck appeared, then disappeared quickly. When he showed himself again he was sneaking through thick brush on an adjacent knoll. I raised my rifle and shot when he paused in a patch of open woods. The hunt was finished, the first day barely an hour old.

The woods echoed with the sounds of rifle fire that day. In the county I hunted, nearly 1,000 hunters took home venison. Many also took back handsome racks. Not only does opening day offer the greatest number of deer, but it also yields some of the heaviest-beamed antlers that will come out of the woods and fields all year.

My buck wouldn't make any record books, but at 138 pounds dressed out, the six-pointer was large for that area and yielded many delicious meals. That buck also did something else. He started a tradition with me of devoting the bulk of my preparation and most intense hunting efforts toward opening day.

I've learned that by hunting hard and exploiting the unique conditions found on opening day, you can greatly improve your chances of killing a buck. By developing a strategy that takes advantage of the potential of this important first day, I've managed to take a buck on every opener I've hunted since that six-point West Virginia deer fell, except when I chose to pass up a small buck in hopes of getting a larger deer later.

The year after taking that six-pointer, I hunted in Virginia and killed a three-pointer that was ambling down Massanutten Mountain. Next I went to West Virginia, and a tall-racked buck tried to ghost past my

stand while light was still so dim on opening day that I was afraid I'd have to pass up the shot. But with the aid of a 2.5X scope, I was able to put a 200-grain bullet behind his shoulder. The deer trotted 40 feet before dropping dead. The following year a seven-pointer fell to my .35-caliber Marlin on the first day.

Last season I hunted Virginia on opening day. Well before light I perched on a comfortable oak branch on a Blue Ridge mountaintop. After passing up a small spike at first light and watching several does slink through the winter woods, I settled the crosshairs of my scoped Remington .30/06 on a thick-beamed, three-point buck. The 150-grain Federal bullet dropped the deer instantly.

A week later West Virginia opened its season. Shortly after dawn a forkhorn tempted me, pussyfooting about within 30 yards of my stand for 10 minutes. I held off, waiting for a larger buck, but for the sixth time in a row the effectiveness of my opening day strategy had proved itself. The techniques allowed me to get within easy range of a standing buck.

On several of the seasons described above, I hunted for a second deer after the opener and failed to get a single shot at another buck. Some years I didn't even see another buck.

Nor was I alone. Those hunters using the later phases of the season face much more dismal prospects for killing a whitetail, particularly in the most heavily hunted states.

But if you have a proved opening-day strategy, you won't have to worry about seeing your odds drop drastically. You'll have your buck in the freezer by the time those low-output days roll around.

Opening day is a rewarding time for several reasons. For starters, except for minimal bowhunting pressure, deer have not been hunted. They've become a bit placid since they last had to contend with hunters, and they've let down their guards a trifle. Not much, mind you. But deer generally become just careless enough to give you a slight advantage when you pursue them on the first day of the season.

On the opener bucks often move in open, easily reached places such as fields and hardwood stands. After the barrage of first-day shots alerts them, most bucks hole up in thick cover where it's all but impossible to find and get clean shots at them. Big bucks travel and feed almost entirely at night after the season opens, bedding for the bulk of the day in overgrown tangles and conifer thickets where hunting quietly is difficult.

Another reason that hunting on opening day is so productive is that many other hunters keep deer moving. For the savvy hunter, that can be an advantage rather than a disadvantage. Few of those other hunters have the patience or willpower to sit still on their stands for more than a few hours. When the itchy hunters move around, they also move deer. Many smiles on opening-day hunters are results of the large number of other hunters milling through the woods, acting unintentionally as part of a huge, unorganized, but very effective drive.

Still, success demands more than simply wandering into the woods and hunkering down on the first stump you see. If things were that simple, more hunters would take deer. In most whitetail states, less than 10 percent of hunters score on the opener.

Among those who take a buck, many are plain lucky. But many opening-day success stories are those of repeat performers. Some hunters score on the first day for eight or 10 seasons in a row.

What do they do that's different from what the typical hunter does? Quite a few things, in most cases. The important differences, though, boil down to two factors: effort and strategy. A strong hunting effort is born of determination, willpower and desire. These are vital for repeated success in the deer woods. But without a strategy, effort will net you only sore muscles and frustration.

Those who succeed on half or more of the openers they hunt have developed a strategy based on the unique circumstances that exist when the season opens. I have two effective approaches. One is to hunt on private land or remote public areas. I can learn the deer's movement patterns before the season and intercept them on opening day without fearing that another hunter will scare them out of their routine.

I like this kind of hunting because it involves pitting my skills as a woodsman and hunter in a one-on-one challenge with a buck. If you hunt this way, you'll take deer that haven't sensed they're being hunted.

The second approach which most hunters will find most useful applies to hunting on crowded grounds. This strategy doesn't involve getting away from the hordes that flock to national forests and wildlife-management areas on the opener, but rather depends on using them to your advantage.

I'll describe this technique in detail later, but let's take a look at the first method. Countless deer that live out their lives more than a mile from the nearest road are never subjected to serious hunting pressure. The sad fact is that few hunters ever venture farther than a quarter-mile from their car. If you're willing to hike in just a mile or two, you can find hunting areas where it's possible to waylay a buck while he's going about his daily routines in a natural way, unpunished by other hunters. You can hunt this way on private and public lands.

To find remote areas, study recent topographic maps. Pinpoint tracts of land that do not have roads within a mile, preferably two or three miles. Get back this far and you're not likely to see another hunter.

It's important, though, to find spots that are not only remote but also choice deer habitat that provides ample food and cover. Look for old homesites, logging trails, clear-cuts, fields, oak ridges edging conifer stands, and new-growth timber.

Scout the area well, as close to opening day as you can. This will give you current information which you need because deer movements alter as foods change and the rut comes on. Tracks, trails, bedding sites, droppings, and scrapes and rubs will help you determine a pattern the deer seem to be using.

For example, deer often feed in fields before and right at daybreak, and then they munch their way through open hardwoods before bedding in thick cover at 8 or 9 A.M. If deer follow this pattern, a logical stand site is in the open hardwoods, preferably where several trails meet and lead into thick cover. You have open shooting in such an area, and you will not likely disturb the deer when you get into your stand before daybreak because they will still be feeding in the fields.

During the rut, hunting over an active scrape or series of them is a good approach. Most bucks visit these sites at least once a day during light hours.

For those who hunt in crowded areas, opening-day prospects can still be bright. But decidedly different tactics are called for than those used by hunters in remote areas. If you hunt where lots of other gunners roam the woods, you want to use them to push a deer to you.

To do this, you should understand how sensitive whitetails are to the presence of humans in the woods. A buck knows his home range the way you know your living room. He hears the commotion early, as the first eager beavers arrive. Car doors click shut, not-so-soft conversation fills the night air, and soon the hunters make their moves, tripping over branches and crunching twigs beneath their boots. The buck scents a heavy mixture of cologne, alcohol, gun oil, and perspiration. If he sticks around, he also sees his pursuers as soon as daylight arrives. Some are late and come wandering in after first light. Others are not dressed warmly enough to stay still on their stands. By 9 or 10 A.M. these hunters start milling around to keep warm.

The deer's three major defense mechanisms—hearing, smell, and sight—have thus been triggered virtually as soon as legal shooting time arrives. A few bucks, mostly young, naive ones, are taken by hunters within a few hundred yards of roads. But most bucks flee these areas of human activity, seeking places where they can hide.

They don't always travel far—just far enough to get away from the commotion and find a thick or difficult-to-reach area where they can feel safe. Dense pine thickets, overgrown swamps, brushy cutover areas, and hard-to-climb craggy ridges all can be used, depending on local terrain.

By studying the layout of public-hunting areas on maps and hiking through them before the season, you can pretty well determine where the deer will go once hunting season starts. *Be there waiting!*

Parking areas indicate where other hunters will be as first light arrives. You can then pinpoint trails that escaping deer will likely use and the heavy cover in which the animals will hide. In some areas it's common to see dozens of whitetails moving toward such hiding spots. By planning ahead, you can dramatically increase your odds of getting a buck over those who enter the woods randomly, relying on luck to send a deer past them.

To get to the best places, sometimes you must walk into the woods hours before daylight. But when you fill your tag, the effort seems worthwhile. Be at your ambush site well before dawn because many bucks, particularly big ones, head for cover early. If you don't see a buck at first light, be patient. More deer will be disturbed and they'll move during midmorning on the opener when hunters start getting cold or bored on their stands and begin moving.

Since a rigorous hike is often required to get into these prime ambush sites near thick hiding cover, it's best to dress lightly at the start and carry extra clothes in a pack on your back. This way you avoid getting overheated and sweating heavily on the trek in, which can create deer-spooking perspiration odors and also leave you shivering in short order once you have to sit still.

I learned this lesson the hard way the first time I hiked up a 2,000-foot peak in the Blue Ridge Mountains of Virginia. The temperature hovered at freezing and a howling wind whipped across the mountainside as I left the pickup in the black of night. The chill factor was down close to zero, so I bundled up to ward off the cold.

A third of the way up I was already warm, and by the time I reached the peak sweat was pouring off me. I loosened my collar and unzipped my coat, but before I could dry out the wind and cold began cutting through me. Wet and chilled, I was forced to give up my stand by midmorning without a buck.

The next time I hiked up that mountain I started earlier so that I could take the hike slowly and avoid breaking into a sweat. Equally important, I wore only a light layer of clothing though the mercury read 25°. I carried the warm clothes I'd need on stand in a backpack.

When I reached the crest of the mountain, I cooled down easily from the climb, broke out the extra clothes, and settled in for a warm, dry watch for deer. Less than two hours later I had my buck.

Though some hunters like driving or stillhunting on opening day, these methods are usually far less productive than hunting from stands. In crowded areas stillhunting, which involves easing slowly through the woods at the same halting pace as a buck, can be dangerous. And if you're moving, you'll seldom be able to see a buck before it sees you since the deer are so fidgety and wary from the sudden influx of humans.

Organized drives usually aren't as effective as standhunting on the first day either. It's hard to tell where other hunters are and how they might interfere with your plans.

By scouting before the season and finding either remote areas where you can hunt undisturbed by the crowds, or by pinpointing the deer's escape havens and allowing other hunters to unwillingly drive the deer to you, chances for scoring on a first-day buck are excellent.

I've outlined the tactics that have put venison in the freezer for me in every recent season I've hunted. If you hunt hard, the same strategies could produce for you. ◆

From Outdoor Life, *October 1981*

SOME FIGURES TO PONDER

I ASKED GAME BIOLOGISTS IN NINE STATES WHAT PERCENTAGES OF THEIR BUCK HARVEST CAME ON OPENING DAY OR IN THE EARLY PART OF THE SEASON. THESE ARE THEIR RESPONSES:

West Virginia. Whitetail deer specialist Thomas Allen put the first-day tally for bucks during the most recent season at 15,730. That was 40 percent of the total buck kill for the 12-day season. The first three days accounted for 69 percent of the bucks.

Michigan. Joel Vogt, a biologist with the Department of Natural Resources, said Michigan hunters account for 33 percent of the total deer harvest on the opener. Translated to the proportion of bucks taken for the season, the opening-day figure rockets to roughly 43 percent of the 96,700 antlered deer taken during the season.

Ohio. Division of Wildlife biologist Dave Urban said 38 percent of the bucks taken in a season are killed the first day.

Georgia. Gib Johnston, chief of information for the state's wildlife agency, told me 33 percent of the deer taken during a recent season were killed on opening day. About 71 percent were killed during the first week of a 7- to 10-week-long hunting period.

New York. The opening-day tally of bucks varies according to region, said Nat Dickenson, big-game unit leader. In the Catskills, 51 percent of the harvest takes place during the first two days of the season. In the heavily hunted central and western parts of the state the figure is 58 percent. In the remote Adirondacks only 9 percent of the harvest occurs during the first two days of the hunting season.

New Jersey. George Howard, chief of the Bureau of Wildlife Management, estimated the first-day take at 30 to 40 percent in south Jersey, where thick scrub oak and pine predominate, and at 60 to 80 percent in the north, where dairy farms are common. Statewide, Howard said 50 to 60 percent of the season's whitetail bucks are downed on the opener.

Pennsylvania. Pennsylvania's opening day buck harvest is usually about 65 percent of the season kill, according to Dale Sheffer, chief of the Division of Game Management.

Alabama. Deer season lasts several months in Alabama, and the limit is one buck a day. The opening-day harvest there is less significant than it is in many other states. Keith Guyse, a biologist with the Department of Conservation and Natural Resources, told me the first-day kill is only 6 or 7 percent of the total 150,000 deer harvest.

Texas. Biologist Fielding Harwell said the deer kill varies from region to region. On the Edwards Plateau, which has one of the highest densities of deer in the United States, 50 percent of the bucks are taken in the first two weeks of a six-week season. In the eastern third of the state, 71 percent of the harvest takes place in the first two weeks. In contrast, hunting in the famous south Texas Brush Country, which yields many trophy bucks, is best during the last two weeks of the season, when 50 percent of the harvest occurs.

Scent Check

by Michael Hanback

It's not enough simply to hunt into the wind. To fool a whitetail's nose, you need to play these five fickle gusts.

◆

A DEER HUNTER IS A TICKING time bomb of scent. Every time he takes a step, shimmies up a tree or shifts on stand—BAM!—a mother lode of molecules explodes from his body and fragments into the air; some of these particles evaporate harmlessly into the environment.

But all too often the scent gremlins surf through the woods on waves of horizontal and vertical air currents until they kick straight up a whitetail's nostrils, igniting that familiar chain reaction: The buck flinches, stamps his foot and sneezes that dreaded alarm, as if to blow the stench back out the way it came. Then it's "see ya," and the deer wheels for cover...for good.

Even though we can't see it or touch it, even if we can't smell it, our scent is very tangible. We emit millions of odor-carrying molecules every day. Skin and hair oils, nasty gases and sweat-bred bacteria slough off our bodies. Even our clothes, boots, bow, arrows, rifle, tree stand and fannypack ooze chemical odors. From a deer's perspective we're like Pigpen, shrouded in a lingering, stinking fog.

So, how do we deal with all that stuff floating around? For starters, keep clean and use odor-neutralizing agents to minimize your scent (see sidebar, page 27). Then play the local winds, hunting where those molecules are driven away from game. In most parts of the country, a westerly wind predominates, which means you can fool many bucks simply by hunting on the eastern sides of food sources, rub lines, scrapes and bedding areas.

It would be nice if things were that cut-and-dried. Instead, we're often confronted with unpredictable zephyrs, swirling gusts, morning and evening thermals and out-and-out gales. Here, then, is how we deal with five fickle winds that spray scent in the most confounding ways.

Light Winds

Whitetails generally move best on days with light winds, when most hunters say, "Cool, no scent to worry about." Think again. Set an open bottle of skunk screen in an airtight room and you'll soon smell a skunk. When you sit in a tree stand for hours on a calm day, your scent likewise diffuses. If you're not careful, a whitetail will soon smell a rat.

Light winds are notorious for kicking up and becoming maddeningly variable—stroking your cheek one minute, lapping the nape of your neck the next. Keep in mind that when a breeze encounters a tree, pocket of brush, lip of a ridge or even a hunter's body, the resulting turbulence swirls scent particles here, there, everywhere.

The conventional thinking is that the best way to fight a finicky wind is to avoid hunting where a buck is leaving arm-size rubs and other heavy sign. The reasoning is that if a big deer winds you in his core area, the jig is up.

That's true, but I'm a firm believer that you need to hunt a mature buck while you have him at least partially patterned, even if the wind is variable and risky. If you don't go now, a food source will dry up, another hunter will move in, a doe a mile away will come into estrus—something will make the deer change his routine so that you never see him again. Grit your teeth, suit up and hope for the best.

Early Thermals

When I'm onto a dominant buck, I like to hunt him in the morning from a tree stand hung along a rub line or scrape-laced funnel well downwind of his bedding area. When the sun comes up and heats the earth, rising bodies of warm air—those ballyhooed thermals—carry my scent particles up, up and away. Then who cares if they swirl in a variable wind? They'll be well above a deer's sniffer if he sneaks in at 7 or 8 A.M.

But while morning thermals work to your advantage most of the time, they can blow your strategy if you hunt too low. Never let warm, rising air carry your scent up and across a sidehill, ridge or bluff where any deer—doe or buck—might appear. As a rule, the higher you can hunt on ridges and hillsides at dawn, the better off you are.

As the day wears on, thermals elevate into what meteorologists call

IS STAND-HUNTING AT DUSK with a gentle breeze in your face the ultimate setup? Not necessarily. As you sit on a stand, your scent slowly tumbles to the ground and spreads out in a widening pool around you, even upwind. If you've been on stand for any length of time and a deer comes moseying in upwind, get ready early—you may have to make some quick decisions on a nervous animal once he whiffs the front edge of your scent pool.

valley winds. The air on ridges and slopes becomes heated by the sun-drenched ground and begins moving up valleys, hollows and canyons. Keep stillhunting and hanging stands high through mid-afternoon, looking for deer approaching away from your scent stream below.

Dusk Flows

One day I hung a tree stand on a rub line midway between a thicket and an oak flat where a Pope and Young 10-pointer prowled. The buck was apt to run the travel corridor either early or late, so I planned to hunt there from 6 A.M. until dark.

He showed at five that evening, drifting off a ridge and meandering my way, angling in from dead upwind. Perfect. I was fixing to draw my bow when the deer jumped like he'd been poked with a cattle prod. He stuck out his nose, inhaled sharply, snorted and wheeled back the way he came. The deer had whiffed the front edge of my scent pool!

As the temperature cools in the evening, the air sinks and hovers in a shallow dome above the ground. What I call "dusk flow" is a nightmare for the tree-stand hunter. It draws his scent particles earthward, where they gather in an ever-widening pool. If a buck comes from virtually any direction and sticks his nose in this pool, you're busted.

After sunset, slopes lose heat and the air cools. Dense, chilly air slides down hillsides and ridges and shoots into the bottoms of valleys and hollows. These so-called mountain breezes can be gusty, picking your scent pool up and depositing it to points below. If you're bowhunting, about the best you can hope for is an evening breeze that blows steadily (at least 5 knots), in which case you'll want to set up downwind and slightly below a feeding area or sign-marked funnel. The wind should push your scent pool away from a buck's nose if he comes in upwind the way he's supposed to.

Gun hunters can deal with dusk flows more effectively, especially if trails and rub lines suggest that deer are moving up and across mountains, hillsides and ridges to feed. At sunset, set up on the lower third of a ridge or in a hollow or creek bottom, where your scent will sink like an anvil, and watch for deer working 50 to 200 yards above, where there's no chance of them winding you.

Heavy Winds

I hate hunting when it's windy—when I can't hear deer hooves popping the leaves several hundred yards away. Is that a doe or a P&Y 10-pointer? The uncertainty of what's coming gets my motor revving.

On a scent-control level, however, there are advantages to hunting in a 10 to 15 mph wind. For one, you can stick a wetted finger into the air and tell with reasonable certainty where your scent fog is headed, then set up accordingly, confident that a buck coming in from the left, right or front won't smell you. Second, since those scent cells are driven fast and in a narrow plume behind you, a deer that angles in slightly downwind might not bust you as he would in a gentler wind. Third, the stronger the wind, the more your scent fog breaks up, especially when it's tossed against ridges, trees and other terrain features. When those molecules explode, it's tough for a deer to pinpoint your location.

One day, while swaying in a tree amid a wind-roiled woodlot, I cut my eyes to a buck in limbo 150 yards away. I raised my binoculars and watched him; nothing moved except his black-tipped nose. That

COMING CLEAN

SURE, IT'S POSSIBLE TO TAKE A NICE DEER EVEN IF YOU'VE GOT YOUR OWN PUNGENT GLAND-THING HAPPENING, BUT MINIMIZING ODOR-CARRYING CELLS WILL MAXIMIZE YOUR SUCCESS. HERE ARE SOME TIPS:

✔ Wash underwear and outerwear in unscented hunter's detergent, line-dry them outside and store in plastic bags.

✔ Shower with unscented soap before each hunt. Use an odor-neutralizing deodorant and body powder. Brush your teeth with baking soda. Afterward, don't eat, smoke or chew while you're on stand.

✔ Cover as much skin as possible to keep cells from escaping into the air. Some hunters swear by charcoal-impregnated Scent-Lok suits. Douse clothes with an odor neutralizer. I've tested Scent Shield, Hunter's Specialties (both in major retailers) and ATSKO brands with good results. Don't forget to spray fannypacks, tree-stand seats, safety belts and other gear.

✔ Wear rubber-bottom boots, which hold and transfer fewer scent molecules to the ground than porous leather boots. Your best option—calf-high rubber boots with the pants tucked in.

✔ Stillhunt or sneak toward stands slowly to minimize sweating. If you're in a hurry, leave your outer layer off until you get on stand and your body begins cooling.

✔ Avoid touching trees, limbs and leaves, minimizing the odds of deer whiffing your lingering scent hours later.

✔ Use a wind-checking device religiously. I prefer a bottle of unscented powder; the white puffs show me what variable winds and vertical air currents are doing.

27

deer worked the wind for 10 minutes, whiffing a bit of my scent. But since most of my fog was rocketing past him, the buck couldn't determine where I was. Finally he decided to head for thick cover, which happened to be on the opposite side of my stand. The deer walked 30 yards below, within cake range of my muzzleloader.

Convection Currents

Ever sat in a tree stand and felt air rotating steadily around you? I'm not talking about a variable wind, but a full-blown convection current.

When two land masses—say a south-facing hillside and a shady creek bottom—are heated unequally by the sun, the air above them roils. The warmer air on the sunny slope is lighter than the cool air in the bottom. The dense, chilly air is drawn to the ground, lifting the warm air up, where it spreads, cools and eventually falls to complete the convective cycle. The circular flow continues as long as the ridge and bottom remain heated unequally.

Sitting in the middle of such a current, your scent fog is in constant motion, the sweeping arc of molecules spooking bucks coming from any direction.

It makes sense not to take a stand at an intersection where two types of terrain are affected in vastly different ways by the sun. It's better strategy to hunt either higher on that sunny slope or deeper back in the shady bottom, where the wind and vertical air flows are more predictable. That's just another way to control the scent gremlins in whitetail country. ◆

From Outdoor Life, *September 1997*

Mock Scrapes & Bogus Branches

by Bob Fratzke,
as told to Glenn Helgeland

When you're after a trophy whitetail,
sometimes it's best to fool Mother Nature.

---◆---

THE TRAP WAS SET: TO GET TO MY mock scrape, the buck had to cross an opening 25 yards from my stand. But just as my pulse started to race, he stopped. As he turned his head slightly, I got a good look at his massive rack, a heavy-looking 12 points.

Staring in the direction of the scrape, the buck put his head down, threw dirt 15 feet with his right front hoof, paused, then threw dirt 15 feet with his left. I could see the hair on his neck stand on end. Then he turned sharply and passed right beneath me.

I drew my bow, followed the deer with my sight pin, and took the shot. The buck ran 30 yards and piled up. When he hit the ground, another large buck ran up to my scrape and then back up the draw.

Now I understood the scene: The buck I shot was trying to get in position for an aggressive move on the second buck, right in front of the scrape I had made the day before.

The results I have achieved using mock scrapes and licking branches have changed my hunting. That's why I've been able to pare down the 40 to 50 stand locations I once had ready for a season to the 10 to 15 stands I concentrate on nowadays. I still scout heavily and spend a lot of time preparing and selecting sites—but now it's more to help bucks select which areas they like best.

I'll never forget the first time I watched a deer just a few yards from me stand and lift its muzzle, roll its eyes back, and sniff and lick a branch I had put in place. That deer's guard was down completely. And I've come to learn that this is common. When bucks approach a mock scrape and licking branch, 9 times out of 10 they don't stop to look around or test the wind. They don't always go directly to the scrape, but more often than not they still present a good shot angle. And after all, a good opportunity is all a hunter can expect.

Perhaps I'm blaspheming Mother Nature a little, but real scrapes are not as reliable as false ones. Some natural scrapes are visited one time only, an outlet for some frustrated buck's increasing breeding urge. Other scrapes may have no licking branch or may not be in the right position for a good shot setup; or they may be in an area that cannot be hunted at all for one reason or another.

But when you make your own scrape, you can make it perfectly: It can be placed to take advantage of the winds and thermals, in front of a stand site that affords you maximum cover and a fairly predictable shooting situation.

How valuable is the licking branch? It's often the catalyst that makes your efforts and a buck's instincts work together for a successful hunt. Bucks and does, both young and adult, use licking branches to leave their scent and check the scents of other deer. They are like calling cards, and every deer is compelled to hand them out. In the spring, when I put in a licking branch and clear the dirt below it, all I'm doing is simulating a scrape that has been there forever. When deer notice the licking branch, they'll come in and change its status from mock to real. By the end of summer, when the rut begins, my licking branches and cleared areas are part of the local herd's natural world.

Scrape areas and licking branches are the deer community's bulletin board. They should be located where activity is highest—where trails meet or change direction sharply, where strips of cover run together along rub lines, along valley bottoms, and on old logging trails. Preexisting scrapes aren't a requirement. If your mock scrape isn't used, it simply means the deer didn't like the setup as well as you did. Reassess the area and try again.

Results often are best when two, three, even four mock scrapes are created at a given location. Whitetails seem to find and take over multiple mock scrapes more quickly and become more excited about them than a single scrape. Once deer take them over, one scrape will be hot for a while, then the deer will move to another scrape, even if it's only a few feet away. They'll continue to rotate from scrape to scrape.

The Setup

Place your stand 10 to 20 yards from the scrape, downwind, in a clump of brush or in front of a big trunk that will help hide you or at least break up your silhouette.

Once the stand is selected, look for a branch of the right height and size to hang over the scrape. Deer like to rub and chew on a single branch tip, so use a thin and sparse one. (Overhanging wild grape vines are the only exception I ever discovered. Deer love them.) The branch tip should be placed five or six feet above the trail, preferably pointing downward.

There are two ways to position the branch: 1) Bend a sapling so that one of its branches is placed downward, using wire to lash it in place. Try to fasten the wire near the base of an anchor tree so the wire is more or less vertical. This makes it a lot easier to bend the sapling to the proper position, and a vertical wire is less dangerous to animals moving through the woods. 2) Cut a small sapling and staple or nail it to a tree near the trail. Position the branch so the limb tip hangs over the trail. Position the branch so the limb tip hangs over the trail at a height that just allows a deer to stretch up and lick it. Wear rubber gloves while doing all this to minimize your scent, and never touch the end of the branch.

Making Your Mock

The soil directly below the branch must also be prepared. Pick a spot with little or no grass. If you can find a totally bare spot, so much the better. Break up the soil surface with a shovel, or if necessary, your boot heel. Clear the earth and make it level. Deer don't like to scrape on a sloped surface.

About one month before the peak of the rut, when bucks start heavy scraping on their own, I begin "sweetening" the soil in the scrapes I've made with a squirt or two of deer urine, even though deer already will have taken over those scrapes. The refreshed scrape is a challenge issued in the dirt, and often one or more bucks already using the scrape will become distinctly less cautious and start showing up earlier or more often to make their own mark.

As far as choosing a deer urine, it hasn't made any difference for me—or to the deer—which type I use. Older supplies have a stronger ammonia smell, but that's basically the odor of all old urine.

If you're male, you might want to experiment with your own urine (hey, you gotta go sometime). I did, and it worked. The mature human male has the hormone testosterone in his urine, which can be attractive to bucks during all stages of the rut, when their own sex hormones are flowing.

As the rut approaches, deer will use the licking branch even more, leaving scent on the branch from saliva and from glands on their foreheads. After using a licking branch, bucks paw the earth below, then leave a smelly signpost in the scrape by urinating on their hocks (over their tarsal glands).

The scent left behind denotes a wealth of information, warning subordinate bucks away and advertising for does. When does are ready to be bred, they will stand expectantly on or next to the scrape. They will remain there 15 to 30 minutes before wandering off if no buck shows up. Does not bred during the first rut will use the scrapes in the same manner 28 days later when they come into season again.

Final Results

During the third week of last October, deer were still coming out to alfalfa fields on the ridgetops where I hunt in the Midwest. On one cold evening that threatened snow the deer were especially active. I passed up three bucks that had checked the mock scrape my stand hung over. Then, at dusk, two does, a couple of minutes apart, moved into and past the scrape. Three minutes later, a 12-pointer walked up, nose to the ground, following the does.

I spent several tense seconds trying to decide whether, this early in the season, the buck was good enough. The buck stood in the scrape, looking toward the does in the field, lifting his head to lick the branch, then looking back again at the field.

I finally decided to shoot, and my 15-yard shot was on target. The buck ran back downhill a short way and fell. I made the right choice—he was a beauty.

In addition to scouting stand sites, taking time to make mock scrapes and licking branches is a rewarding way to kick-start the action. And any time you can find a way to get closer to whitetail bucks, you're on the right track—or at least the right mock scrape and licking branch. ◆

From Outdoor Life, *September 1995*

In the Presence of Game

by Robert Willis

Knowing how to react when a deer is in range may be hunting's toughest skill.

◆

T HE HUNTER SAT with his back to a tree, watching his frosted breath slowly drift on the still morning air.

Daybreak had come two hours ago, a hickory root, unseen in the predawn darkness, dug into his hip. The sound of an occasional shot in the distance made him increasingly antsy. He looked up and down the ridge. "This is a good stand," he told himself for the fourth time. Two deer trails converged in a single path 40 yards in front of him. A fresh scrape lay right where the trails joined. He could see for 60 yards up and down the ridge. Anything coming from either direction would be his.

A twig popped softly behind him. That was no squirrel! He turned quickly to the right and peered around the tree trunk, straight into the face of a buck 39 yards away. The deer locked eyes with the hunter...and was gone. The

hunter leaped to his feet and fired in vain at the white flag disappearing into the undergrowth. He threw this cap on the ground in disgust.

A mile away another hunter sat leaning against a tree, listening to the echoes of the fusillade from the valley below. This hunter sat at the edge of an abandoned logging road and had a clear view for 100 yards to the left and 30 yards to the right, where the road went through a low gap in the ridge, a natural crossing spot for deer. A well-used trail lay atop the ridge in front of and slightly above him. As the hunter pondered the distant shots, he heard a soft sound behind him. He froze, listening. A stick snapped, behind and slightly to his right. The thick bole of trees screened him from that direction, so he carefully turned this head and waited. In a few heartbeats a buck appeared, climbing steadily up the hillside toward the gap. The hunter's rifle lay across his knees, its muzzle pointing to the left. It would take the buck at least a minute to reach the gap, so he began to ease the gun slowly across his body. By the time the buck reached

the edge of the road the hunter had twisted his body 90 degrees to the right and brought the stock against his cheek. He lay the sights on the deer's moving shoulder, and just as the buck stepped into the open road, he firmly pushed off the safety. The faint metallic click reached the deer's sensitive ears and stopped it. The buck never heard the shot that killed it.

Two hunters, each with a similar opportunity. Both had scouted before the season. Both had selected excellent stands. Yet one got to test the edge on his new skinning knife while the other got nothing but a bruise from a hickory root. Why? The successful hunter knew how to handle himself in the presence of game.

Knowledge First

Knowing what to do when a buck appears is the most difficult thing to learn about whitetail hunting. There is no teacher like experience, but experience requires opportunity, which we have already said is rare.

Let's say the buck of your dreams is moving in on you, and you have to get off an accurate shot without spooking him. The problems you face when the buck is in sight are the same whether you are standhunting, stillhunting, or stalking. If you're lucky, he'll pass out of sight behind something and you can quickly and quietly raise your rifle, taking the shot when he steps back into view. But if he is moving through open woods, any quick movement will catch his eye every time. The trick is to match the speed of your movements to the speed of the deer.

To a deer moving through the woods, everything around it seems to move as well. To better understand this, find a spot where you can walk 20 or 30 yards without having to watch where you step, and look to one side as you walk along. That's how a deer's visual radar works. Its eyes are set on the sides of its head, and looking to the side will give you a better feel for what it sees. In this two-dimensional side view you'll notice as you move that every object in the woods changes its position in relation to everything else. Trees move behind and out of your line of vision as others come into view; brushy thickets open up to real clearings and then close again; hillsides rise or fall away. The faster you walk, the faster these things change. And vice versa.

It's the same for that approaching buck. If you can judge, and match, his speed by moving your gun and body at about the same rate that everything else around him is changing position, he is unlikely to detect the motion. The farther away a buck is, and the sharper the angle at which he's traveling with respect to your location, the faster you can move. The toughest deer to move against is the one that comes straight at you; your position won't shift much in his eyes.

Use all the time you have. The most difficult part is keeping your cool and forcing yourself not to hurry, especially when the rifle butt is almost at your shoulder.

The deer's body language can also help you determine how to make your move. If it has recently been spooked by another hunter, it will be looking for danger. If it's just traveling from one place to another, you'll have a little more leeway in your movements. The key is the deer's head position. An undisturbed deer carries its head rather low and out in front of its body. One that is on the alert will usually have its head stuck straight in the air. When really spooked, a deer sometimes crouches and moves along with its belly to the ground like a stalking cougar.

A rutting buck following a doe in heat is the easiest mark. When you see one with his neck stretched out, upper lip curled back, and tail stuck straight out behind him, you can stand up and sing "Born in the USA" without making him jump. But don't forget the doe; if she sees you and bolts, she'll pull the buck with her.

Above all, never make eye contact with your quarry. Nothing alarms a wild creature more than looking into the eyes of a predator at close range. If you think you've been seen, look at some other part of the deer's anatomy—nose, antlers, shoulder—anything but the eyes.

Okay, you've been rattling or calling and you're successful. Here comes a good buck. But he's close, and it's far too late to shift your body without being detected. It is sometimes much easier to switch sides with the gun than to try to move your entire body without being spotted. Shooting off the opposite shoulder isn't as difficult as it sounds. The target will be close and is fairly large, and a few shots fired on the range before opening day will give you the confidence you need to pull it off cleanly. Just remember, though, if you have any doubts, you owe it to the game to pass up the shot.

Coming out a winner in that long-anticipated confrontation with a big buck is 50 percent planning, 50 percent reaction. Mental preparation and a solid knowledge of the ways of game build confidence and ultimately lead to success. Knowing how to keep your cool will not only increase your take, but you will find that you understand and take pride in being in the presence of game, no matter the outcome of the hunt. ◆

From Outdoor Life, *November 1995*

Working Stiffs

by Charles J. Alsheimer

A deer decoy could be the best hunting partner
you've ever had.

———————— ◆ ————————

IT'S NO STRETCH TO SAY THAT THE
use of deer decoys—call it "deer-
coying"—is the hottest thing to come
along in whitetail hunting in the last 25
years. Well, at least the last 10. Back in
1988, a request for a deer decoy at your
local sports shop was likely to draw a
bewildered shrug from the man behind
the counter, but in recent years that same
man probably helped sell more than
500,000 deer decoys to hunters across the
country. And this year alone, another
100,000 decoys are expected to move off
the shelf. Can you say "growth industry"?

I began using decoys for both photography and hunting shortly after the Flambeau Co. came out with the first three-dimensional decoy in 1989. My initial impression was, "This is too easy." But then I was brought back to earth with a string of disappointing hunts. I realized that I had been enjoying a measure of beginner's luck. The last eight years have taught me that for decoying to be effective, several factors have to work in concert. If just one is left out, your chances of success fall off sharply.

The Setup

I can't tell you how many times I've set up a decoy in thick cover only to watch a deer walk past without ever seeing it. The first rule of decoying is to place your decoy where deer can readily see it, ideally at the edge of a field or in a well-traveled funnel.

Because three-dimensional decoys can be cumbersome and noisy to

AS THIS AMOROUS WHITETAIL SO explicitly demonstrates, a decoy's gender determines how deer will approach it. In short, a buck will ease up on a doe decoy from behind, but will confront a buck decoy head-on. Which simply means that doe decoys should be placed upwind and facing away from your stand, while buck decoys should be positioned facing toward you. Either scenario will draw approaching bucks past your stand.

assemble, think through how you're going to get them into hunting position. Nothing ruins a hunting site faster than hollow plastic parts snapping together, so do the assembling at least 100 yards from where you intend to hunt. Also, never, never leave a decoy set up when you're not hunting over it. It takes just once for a deer to be fooled by a decoy before your chances of fooling him again drop to practically nil.

There are three other pre-hunt keys to keep in mind: First, free the decoy of any human odor by spraying it liberally with a cover-up scent. Second, make sure the decoy is anchored to the ground. The last thing you need is your decoy talking a tumble in a wind gust, or from a real deer's gentle nudge.

Finally, never carry a decoy without wearing Blaze Orange—on you and the deke. Today's decoys are extremely lifelike, and safety is a primary concern when transporting them.

Silhouette or 3-D?

Both three-dimensional and silhouette decoys have their place. The obvious advantage of silhouettes is that they're light, which makes them perfect for hunters who have to schlepp in deep to their stands. The equally obvious disadvantage is that if a deer gets close to a silhouette decoy and begins circling it, the party's over. In most cases the deer will spook and bolt. So if you're going to use a silhouette, lean it up against a brush pile or stake it at the end of a field where you're trying to draw deer from across the clearing.

Three-dimensional decoys are cumbersome and more expensive, but well worth the money and their extra weight. They can lure a buck right into your lap—provided you mind the details.

Buck or Doe Decoy?

Both doe and buck decoys work best from two weeks before breeding until the end of the rut. Doe decoys are almost always the better option. The only exception occurs when there's an abundance of mature bucks, which results in a high aggression factor in the local herd. If your hunting area is blessed with such a problem, put antlers on your decoy.

When bowhunting with a doe decoy, place it 20 to 25 yards upwind and facing away or quartering away from you. Here's why: Generally a buck will circle in behind a doe decoy, rather than come straight in. And if a buck suspects something is odd about the scene (which he often does), he'll hang up 20 to 30 yards out from the decoy. If the deke is about 25 yards from your stand, you might be able to get a shot when the buck hangs up, quite often at almost point-blank range. Should the buck come all the way to the decoy you'll still have many opportunities for a broadside shot while he explores its backside.

If you're bowhunting with a buck decoy, place it about 20 yards upwind of your stand, positioned so it's facing or quartering toward you. Bucks will almost always approach a buck decoy from the front, a tendency that should put you in prime shooting position if the decoy's facing your stand.

The decoy's antlers should be representative of the region you're hunting. In highly pressured areas where there are few mature bucks, that means nothing larger than a 100-class Boone and Crockett set of antlers. Bucks judge each other by body size, antler size or a combination of these factors. This sets the tone for their aggression. You might try using just a single antler on a buck decoy, which might suggest to other whitetails that the deke is a fighter, thus stimulating an attack.

One last note: If you're bowhunting over a buck decoy and an approaching buck is one you want to take (and shows an aggressive attitude), you'll have to shoot him before he reaches the fake. Even if the opponent is plastic, the frenzy of a fight will make a shot impossible. Besides, you're protecting property here—a decoy is never quite the same once you have to duct tape its head back on.

From Outdoor Life, *October 1997*

Crazy Week Whitetails

by Charles J. Alsheimer

In the days leading up to the peak of the whitetail rut, bucks go bonkers. Hormones have the animals in a frenzy, and the hunting is never better.

WHEN I WAS GROWING UP ON a farm, sage hunters always talked about mid-November and the whitetail rut. And I, like so many other hunters, bought into the idea that the best time to hunt whitetails was during the peak, which in my country was from November 10 to 25. Certainly this is an excellent time to

hunt big bucks. But there is an even more productive time to hunt whitetails, especially trophy bucks.

Just before the peak of the whitetail rut there is a period of time I call the crazy week. It often lasts from seven to 10 days, and during this time whitetail bucks go absolutely ballistic. When bucks are caught up in the frenzy of the crazy week, all kinds of opportunities open to the hunter who has done his homework.

Technically, a whitetail buck can breed does from the time it peels velvet until its antlers are cast in the late winter. But it takes two to tango, and north of the 40th parallel (which runs through the Pennsylvania/Maryland border in the East and through northern California in the West), the majority of does do not come into estrus until mid- to late November.

RUT DATA

STATE	RANGE	PEAK
ALABAMA	Oct. 25-Feb. 21	Jan.
ARIZONA	Nov.-Feb.	Mid Jan.
ARKANSAS (north)	Oct. 21-Dec. 17	Nov. 5
(central)	Oct. 15-Jan. 1	Nov. 15
(south)	Oct. 25-Feb. 6	Nov. 27
COLORADO	Oct. 15-Dec. 15	Nov. 15-30
CONNECTICUT	Oct.-Jan.	Nov. 15-30
DELAWARE	Oct.-Dec.	Nov. 1-21
FLORIDA (north)	Oct.-Dec.	Oct.15-Nov. 15
(northwest)	Jan.-Apr.	Feb. 10-Mar. 15
(central)	Sept.-Nov.	Sept. 20-Oct. 20
(south)	July-Oct.	July 20-Aug. 20
(Keys)	Sept.-Feb.	Oct.
GEORGIA (coastal)	Sept.-Jan.	Early Oct.
(north)	Sept.-Jan.	Late Nov.
(midwest)	Oct.-Dec.	Mid Nov.
(southeast)	Sept.-Dec.	Late Oct.
IDAHO	Oct. 21-Nov. 28	Nov. 10-25
ILLINOIS	Oct.-Dec.	Nov. 10-20
INDIANA	Oct.-Dec.	Nov. 1-20
IOWA	Oct.-Jan.	Nov. 2-23
KANSAS	Oct.-Feb.	Nov. 15-30
KENTUCKY	Oct. 15-Dec. 15	Nov. 5-20
LOUISIANA (east)	Nov.-Feb.	Dec.-Mid Jan.
(northwest)	Sept.-Jan.	Mid Oct.-Mid Nov.
(southwest)	Aug.-Dec.	Mid Sept.-Oct.
MAINE	Oct.-Dec.	Nov. 15-30
MARYLAND	Oct.-Dec.	Oct. 21-Nov. 10
MASSACHUSETTS	Oct.-Jan.	Nov. 5-22
MICHIGAN	Oct.-Jan.	Mid Nov.
MINNESOTA	Sept. 15-Feb.	Nov. 1-15
MISSISSIPPI	Nov. 20-Mar. 15	Dec. 5-Jan. 15
MISSOURI	Oct.-Jan.	Nov. 10-25
MONTANA	Oct.-Dec.	Mid Nov.
NEBRASKA	Oct.-Feb.	Nov. 8-Dec. 12
NEW HAMPSHIRE	Oct.-Dec.	Nov. 15-25
NEW JERSEY (north)	Oct.-Jan.	Nov. 1-17
(south)	Oct.-Jan.	Nov. 10-30
NEW MEXICO	Nov.-Feb.	Dec. 21-Jan. 7
NEW YORK	Sept.-Jan.	Nov. 10-30
NORTH CAROLINA	Oct.-Dec.	Nov. 7-15
NORTH DAKOTA	Oct. 15-Jan. 20	Nov. 20-Dec. 10
OHIO	Oct.-Jan.	Nov. 1-15
OKLAHOMA	Oct.-Dec.	Nov. 18-25
OREGON (east)	Nov. 1-Dec. 15	Nov. 10-30
(west)	Nov. 1-Dec. 30	Nov. 15-30
PENNSYLVANIA	Oct.-Jan.	Nov. 5-20
RHODE ISLAND	Oct.-Dec.	Nov. 10-25
SOUTH CAROLINA	Sept.-Dec.	Oct. 15-Nov. 15
SOUTH DAKOTA	Oct.-Jan.	Nov. 18-Dec. 7
TENNESSEE	Oct.-Jan.	Nov. 15-Dec. 15
TEXAS (south)	Nov.-Feb.	Dec. 15-Jan. 10
(central and north)	Oct.-Jan.	Nov. 1-30
VERMONT	Nov.-Dec.	Nov. 15-25
VIRGINIA	Oct.-Jan.	Nov. 1-17
WASHINGTON	Nov. 1-Dec. 10	Nov. 20-Dec. 7
WEST VIRGINIA	Oct.-Jan.	Nov. 10-23
WISCONSIN	Oct.-Jan.	Nov. 1-15
WYOMING	Oct.-Dec.	Nov. 15-Dec. 7

RUT DATA - Range and peak periods can vary due to complex and interrelated factors of population dynamics: sex ratio, herd density and buck age structure; and nutritional influences: forage, mast crop, weather and carrying capacity.

In September whitetail bucks start rubbing their antlers, and sparring activity increases. As September blends into October, bucks begin making scrapes, and by mid-October a few whitetail does come into estrus and are bred. This causes what I refer to as a false rut because there aren't enough does in heat to go around. This builds frustration among the bucks and releases a flurry of rutting activity.

Research by wildlife biologist J. M. McMillin has shown that a whitetail buck's testicular volume and serum testosterone level peak around November 1. As a result, bucks are seemingly overflowing with hormones by late October. With few does in estrus, they begin covering as much ground as it takes to find breedable does. Rubbing, scraping and doe chasing reach a fever pitch as November arrives. The crazy week begins.

During the crazy week, whitetail bucks, large and small, let their guard down as their sex drive overtakes them. Because does are not yet willing to breed, and flee the aggressive pursuit, bucks are often alone as they travel their territory. They also become less nocturnal and more careless as they relentlessly search for receptive does.

The crazy week ends when the bulk of does come into estrus. Almost overnight, rubbing and scraping activities diminish as the breeding begins. Receptive does are abundant and a buck will often "hole up" with a doe for up to 72 hours.

Several years ago I had a ringside seat to this hole-up phenomenon while shooting photographs on a large estate which was off-limits to hunting. It was mid-November. An inch of snow covered the ground, and the rut was nearing its peak. Around noon, while I was sitting next to a blowdown, a big 10-point buck trailed a doe through a clearing 50 yards from me. The doe was not yet in estrus, so she went under a deadfall to escape the buck's advances. For the next three hours the buck chased off seven different bucks who also had been attracted to the female. Before the day was over I photographed the buck breeding the doe while all seven bucks watched from a distance.

When I came back the next day the eight bucks were still near the doe. Their breeding instincts were heated, and the presence of this doe was the driving force in their minds. This is typical behavior during the peak of the rut, and an important factor when hunting. If a hunter does not have a hot doe in his neighborhood during the peak of the rut, there is a high probability the area will be devoid of bucks until a doe in heat moves in.

The key to pinpointing the crazy week is knowing when the white-tail rut peaks. Substantial research has determined whitetail breeding dates across the country, and the crazy week generally begins seven to 10 days before peak breeding dates.

A study by wildlife biologist Robert McDowell pinpointed peak whitetail breeding dates based on latitude. McDowell's study revealed that the farther south one goes, the less predictable the whitetail rut becomes.

For the most part, below the 36th parallel (south of North Carolina) the rut is drawn out. Breeding can start as early as August and last until February.

There are exceptions, however, and south Texas is one of them. During the last three years, I've killed four whitetails in the 140 Boone and Crockett Club point class in far south Texas, where the peak of the rut is around Christmas. All four were taken during the crazy week phase from December 14 to 20. One I rattled in, and the others were taken while they were on the move.

In the whitetail-rich provinces of Canada, which lie above the 48th parallel, the whitetail rut is later in November and condensed into a short time. In the whitetail's Northern range, the crazy week's peak can fall anywhere from November 10 to 15. So, although rut dates vary from state to state, my experience reveals that the crazy week exists, in varying degrees, throughout the continent. A tool every serious whitetail hunter should have is the "Whitetail Deer Population Map." The map shows both deer densities throughout the United States and each state's rut dates.

As a hunter and photographer I live for the crazy week and plan my photography and hunting around it. I'm primarily a scrape hunter, and I set my stands near these markers. I incorporate a number of techniques to go along with scrape hunting. Buck scent lures, rattling and grunting are techniques I love. However, scouting and setting up my ambush are what make the other strategies work.

Scraping begins and increases in late October and early November at the onset of the crazy week. During this time I try to look for two things. I search for areas frequented by several doe groups—the more the better. The does will become buck magnets as the rut approaches. I also look for transition zones, the areas lying between feeding and bedding sites. In the process I attempt to zero in on the most heavily used scrape—called a primary scrape—in the area's transition zone.

I also try to find the primary scrape (or scrapes) in areas offering a fair amount of cover, because bucks tend to visit them more during daylight hours. Once the crazy week arrives, a primary scrape located in a transition zone will become a hub of activity as lovesick bucks search for breedable does.

From mid-October until the peak of the rut I try to make the primary scrape as attractive as possible. To keep a whitetail buck interested in a scrape I place a scent canister above the licking branch. To keep things fresh, I add scent to the can every other day and also put a little scent in the scrape.

I place my tree stand 40 to 60 yards from the scrape and select a tree surrounded by fairly thick cover. The thick vegetation enables me to camouflage my movements better when rattling. I don't try to set up closer than 40 yards from a scrape because most mature bucks merely scent-check a scrape during daylight hours rather than walking right to it. This placement puts me in a better position to intercept the buck as he moves by the scrape.

November 4, 1989, in New York state was the type of day every bowhunter looks forward to: cool, overcast and no wind, perfect for a crazy week experience. At about 2:30 P.M. I headed for my stand. About 75 yards from it, I applied buck lure to the bottom of my rubber boots and proceeded to make a scent trail through the woods. I quietly walked 50 yards past the stand before backtracking and climbing into the tree stand. Fifty yards away in a grove of white pines was a very active scrape I had been doctoring for more than two weeks.

My plan was to wait about a half-hour, go through a rattling sequence, then wait another hour before rattling again. At 3 P.M. I rattled aggressively for about five minutes then hung the antlers on a branch. Nothing responded.

For the next hour only chickadees and gray squirrels kept me company. At 4:00 P.M. I stood up and rattled again. I didn't have to wait long for action. To my right I heard a twig snap in the nearby pine thicket. I wasn't sure what it was but felt confident it was a deer or coyote responding to the rattling. Slowly I raised my grunt tube and grunted softly once.

A beautiful eight-pointer walked out of the pines with his nose on the ground and tail outstretched. He was following the scent trail I had laid down more than an hour before. Twenty-five yards from me he stopped and curled his lip to enhance his sense of smell. He walked five yards ahead into an opening. In one motion, I came to a full draw and released my arrow. My aim looked true and on impact the big buck bolted and ran back into the pines.

After calming down, I climbed from the stand and went to where the buck was standing when I shot. From the blood-covered arrow lying on the ground I knew the hit was good, and after a short tracking effort I came upon the eight-pointer. The buck went less than 75 yards before going down.

Preparation played a big part in the hunt's success, and my use of rattling, grunting and buck lure techniques made the experience very special. But the real key to my success was the crazy week.

A mature whitetail buck is no pushover and requires all the hunting savvy a hunter can muster. For roughly 50 weeks a year a buck lives on the edge and cannot survive by making mistakes. But once a year his body chemistry overtakes him and his urge to breed becomes overpowering. During this time, whitetail bucks are on a mission and in the process create the crazy week.

For the serious whitetail hunter the crazy week is the ultimate. From south Texas to Alberta, it provides hunters one of the most exciting hunting situations on earth, the chase phase of the whitetail rut. ◆

From Outdoor Life, *October 1992*

CRAZY CONDITIONS

*A*LTHOUGH RUT DATES ARE FAIRLY PREDICTABLE FROM A BIOLOGICAL STANDPOINT, THE WHITETAIL'S COAT, THE MOON AND THE WEATHER CAN PLAY AN IMPORTANT PART IN PINPOINTING THE PEAK OF THE CRAZY WEEK.

By the time late October rolls around, whitetails have their winter coat. If the first of November arrives and it is unseasonably warm, bucks will move very little during daylight hours because their system simply cannot stand the heat. It's kind of like a person wearing a down coat in 90° temperatures.

During periods of warm weather, the craziness will take place only during the coolness of night. Because of this, I've become a weather watcher. Wherever I hunt the crazy week I hope for cool temperatures and a rapidly rising or falling barometric pressure. When cool weather fronts dovetail with the whitetail's peak hormonal level, the result is sheer excitement in the woods.

My experience has shown that the effect moon phases have on the crazy week depends on where one hunts. In the North, where the whitetail rut is condensed, a full moon seems to have little effect on a buck's movement during daylight hours. Once northern whitetails start their breeding frenzy, the only thing that seems to affect their movement is warm weather, which will decrease their daytime activity, and heavy rainfall, which can slow down rutting activity.

But in the South, where the rut is drawn out, a full moon can increase the deer's nocturnal activity. On days following a moonlit night, hunting tends to be slow in the morning and evening. However, it has been my experience that buck activity during midday is considerably higher in such areas during the full-moon phase.

Tough Talk

by Michael Hanback

No hype. No hoopla. Just the plain truth
about calling in trophy whitetails.

FOR 20 DAYS MY RATTLES AND grunts had fallen on deaf ears, but on the 21st morning I played the concerto anyway. *Bravo!* A buck tuned in and thought enough of what he heard to approach my stand—eyes darting and ears rolling like tiny satellite dishes. I've shot whitetails with bigger racks, but this one was special. After weeks of failure, I was once again a maestro.

For all the hype, deer calling remains a dark science. It doesn't work all the time, or even most of the time, but if you keep playing the horns and piping the tubes, you should strike a chord with a few bucks each fall. And when one hears what he likes and comes crashing to the sound, it's enough to make your season.

Rattle Traps

Clashing a set of horns (antlers, to you literal types) falls under a secondary definition of "call" in *Webster's Tenth*—"to command or request to come." By imitating two deer tangling with their racks, you might command a buck to your stand, be it an inquisitive young animal lured by the ruckus, or an old, hip-swaying bruiser looking for two rivals battling over a doe.

Rattling was originated in Texas decades ago, and there the technique keeps on producing awesome results. On intensively managed ranches where buck-to-doe ratios are maintained near one-to-one, there's keen competition among the 4½- to 6½-year-old bucks for the favors of those relatively few does. When the rut is right, you can cruise around a ranch and hit the horns from several spots and expect 5 to 10 big deer to zoom in each day.

But if you hunt where the buck-to-doe ratio is not so balanced— where fewer mature bucks live per square mile and where the hunting pressure is less controlled—things are a bit different. First, get it through your skull that you ain't gonna rattle up 10 bucks a day, or even 5. In fact, unless you're a virtuoso with the horns, you might not call up that many in a season. Which means you better play that tune right.

Up until two weeks prior to the peak of the rut, use your rattling horns to simulate bucks that are simply horsing around or testing each other's dominance. "Spar" in 30- to 90-second intervals—ticking and rubbing the horns or working a rattle bag or box moderately hard. Many days, I "blind spar" every 30 minutes or so. While hard rattling will sometimes spook a young buck skulking in the foliage, sparring is far less intimidating and might bring him in. In fact, sparring can pique the interest of any deer—no matter what his age—and pull him toward your post.

The ultimate reward of rattling is when an old 8- or 10-pointer comes charging in with wild eyes, raised hackles and an overall demeanor that screams, "I'm gonna kick some butt!" Late in the pre-rut is the time to mimic the mother of all deer fights. For 10 days or so before the does come into heat, sex-starved bucks prowl around like bullies on the block, rolling in to watch, or even join, a good brawl. "Five- or six-year-old bucks lock antlers and try to kill each other," says Gary Roberson, owner of Burnham Brothers Calls and one of the country's premier horn rattlers. "There's awesome pushing and shoving, with dirt flying everywhere. Each deer tries to flip the other and horn him on the ground. The loser often runs off crippled, with the winner hooking him in the butt."

While no human can rattle with such genuine ferocity, do the best you can. Hammer those horns. Sequence-wise, most anything goes so long as it sounds like a fight. Roberson has a favorite. "There's not much rattle-and-stop, rattle-and stop," he says. "Once big deer lock up, it's mostly grinding."

When working the horns from a ground blind, go for broke; use the antlers to rake bushes, sling leaves and chuck dirt. Thump them on the ground to imitate deer stomping. Bucks often knock the air out of each other as they push and shove, so mix in some aggressive grunts.

To grab the attention of bucks prowling nearby, Roberson is a wild man with the rattling horns. He'll keep going for two to three minutes, but I opt for 30- to 60-second bursts of grinding, which I feel is more in line with the actual way deer battle. "Most fights between mature deer last 30 seconds or less," even the frenetic Roberson admits.

CALLING TACTICS

✔ CALL WHERE BUCKS are most apt to hear you—near feeding areas on afternoon hunts; downwind of bedding thickets in the morning; in strips of woods, creek bottoms and similar funnels any time of day.

✔ GRIND, GRUNT AND ESTROUS BLEAT in thickets laced with doe trails and blazed with buck rubs and scrapes.

✔ A RUT-CRAZY BUCK may charge across an open field to check out calls, but most of the time it's best to set up in broken cover, where a big deer can pick his way toward your stand.

✔ SNEAK QUIETLY into an area and call with the wind in your face. But watch your sides and back. Sometimes bucks circle in downwind, trying to smell the rattling, grunting or bleating "deer."

✔ CALL WITH THE SUN over your shoulder, which makes it easy to catch the flash of incoming antlers and hide. Additionally, a buck that looks into the sun is less apt to see you grinding horns or raising a tube.

✔ IN BIG COUNTRY, covering lots of acres can better your odds of striking deer. Rattle and grunt from a ground blind, then wait 30 minutes. If no buck shows, stillhunt deeper into the cover, then start the sequence again.

✔ WHEN HUNTING SMALL WOODLANDS and thickets, try calling from a tree stand. You're immobile, but then that's probably best given the conditions—you're not pushing deer off the property.

✔ BUCKS HOMING IN ON CALLS look long and hard. Wear head-to-toe camo when bowhunting. In gun season, don safety orange and set up where you're visible to another hunter who may come to your sounds.

✔ AFTER EACH ROUTINE, drop the horns or tubes and freeze as you scan the cover. Calling won't work if you move around and spook bucks that are on the way.

"One buck quickly realizes the other is stouter, so he breaks and runs."

When the rut explodes, many hunters hang up the horns, thinking there's no way they can call a dominant buck away from an estrous doe. Maybe so, but I keep rattling anyway. Plenty of frustrated "beta" bucks with good-size racks roam the woods, and one of them might sneak a peek at your calls. And who knows, you might even rattle up an "alpha" deer between does.

Continue working the horns into the post-rut as well. Bucks may be weary from all that chasing and breeding, but they're still looking for fun. If a big deer thinks a battle has erupted over an unbred doe, he might step over for a look at what's in it for him.

When in Doubt, Grunt

If you could follow a buck around the woods, you'd find that he grunts a lot more often than you might think. He's not just talking to himself.

"Deer grunt for many reasons," says David Hale, the call maker from Kentucky. "They may be lost, or they may just want to socialize. Bucks grunt out of aggression and when chasing does. When you call, you may be saying any number of things that appeal to a buck."

There's been much said recently about "specific" vocalizations—that does and immature bucks pipe high-pitched grunts, while mature bucks utter guttural calls. This is correct...sometimes. I've heard monster deer with trilling grunts. And last fall a spike cruised by my stand, grunting like a market hog. Who can say what's right? When I grunt, all I try to do is sound like a deer. This is not to say that I won't vary the tones in my call. I will—and often—either by using a single adjustable tube or by blowing a couple of different devices. Think of it like turkey calling: Just as a tom might like a whistling diaphragm over a raspy box, a buck may come to either piping or throaty grunts. You'll do well to offer a buck his options.

During the pre-rut—and the post-rut for that matter— you have nothing to lose and possibly a lot to gain by blowing "contact" grunts throughout the day. For an idea of how the call sounds, huff air up from your diaphragm while saying *ecc, ecc* or *ack, ack* and hold each tone for half a second. When on stand, grunt like that every 10, 20 or 30 minutes, whatever feels right. The idea is simply to contact a buck and reel him in.

As the rut approaches, scale up to more animated grunts. Call them what you like—tending, aggression or cackle grunts—but the sequences are the same. Blow fast, choppy streams of *ack, ack, ack, ack,* punctuated by a loud, distorted *urrrrg, urrrg.* Five-second sequences are common, but grunt longer if you like. A horny buck may come to what he thinks is a rival running a doe, or an interloper busting for trouble.

While you might get lucky with blind calling, grunting is most effective on bucks you can see or hear. Let's say you detect a buck grunting in some foliage. Call to him immediately—he's right there and looking to hook up with another deer.

Here's something that happens a lot: You spot a buck slipping into a thicket or cresting a ridge just out of range. Now's the time when

HOT CALLS

OLID SHEDS OR ANTLERS SAWED FROM A BUCK SHOT YEARS AGO WORK WELL FOR RATTLING. USE MEDIUM-SIZE HORNS WITH DECENT MASS.

Each beam should also have a couple of "grinding tines" 6 to 8 inches long. Saw off brow points to keep from mashing your fingers.

Some people say bucks can tell the "ring" of fake antlers. Phooey! I've rattled in several deer with synthetics such as Primos's Fightin' Horns which are well-balanced and have six perfectly molded grinding tines.

Rattling boxes and rattling bags are a breeze to use, especially in a tree stand. I find them best for sparring and moderately hard grinding. Check out Lohman's Fighting Bucks box and the Rattling Bag from Hunter's Specialties.

I've tested hundreds of grunt tubes, most of which sound enough like a deer to work. I do recommend a full-size grunter with an expandable tube, like that found in 1) Primos's Hyper Buck and Doe, 2) Lohman's "Touch Tone" Deer Call and 3) Quaker Boy's Phantom Buck and Doe. Knight & Hale's Extend-A-Tone is another excellent grunt tube. While blowing the call, work the tube to utter a nice mix of high-pitched and guttural grunts.

you have absolutely nothing to lose. Grunt sharply. If the deer hears you, even at a distance of 100 yards, or farther on a windless day, he'll stop and look at least half the time. And if you have the crosshairs on him, that might be all the break you need.

If a buck stops for an instant but then continues walking, call again, this time a little louder. You might also ease up the horns and try some sparring. A combination of grunting and rattling can be the magic chord that turns a buck back your way. If he does turn, stop calling. The deer is homing in on the sound with rolling ears and eyes the size of cue balls. If you grunt or rattle again, there's a good chance he'll see you and spook. Or he may just hang up, looking for the deer making all that racket. Don't risk it: Once a buck starts your way, just let him come, and if he loses interest and veers off, only then should you grunt some more.

One time, a big 8-pointer cruised within 20 yards of my bow stand and froze behind some honeysuckle. When the buck looked away, I sneaked up my tube and grunted. The curious buck moved out into a shooting lane you could drive a Mack through, and I thought, "Gotcha!" But he kept on trucking. I grunted again. He wheeled and skidded to a stop...behind an oak tree. I called once more, then drew. I loosed my arrow to his lungs as he motored back across the lane.

The following scenario is played out thousands of times across the country each season. A hunter calls for weeks, or even months. Nothing. Nada. Then one day he grunts and a buck walks into his lap. The message? Simple. Keep playing your tune until you bring down the house.

From Outdoor Life, *November 1997*

When You Jump a Buck

by Tim Jones

The next time you see those white flags fly, don't give up and don't curse out loud; you'll spook them. After all, the hunt isn't over, it's only just begun.

◆

YOU BLEW IT! YOU WERE OUT prowling the deer woods, let your attention lapse for a moment, and took one step too many. Suddenly, there it was, a white tail bounding away through the brush, looking as big and bright as a freshly washed bed sheet waving in the wind.

Your heart is pounding, your hands are shaking, and you feel like calling yourself every name in the book for not seeing that deer first. If only you'd moved a little slower, paid more attention, been looking in the right direction. Don't start cursing—at least not aloud. You still have a very good chance of seeing that deer again and perhaps even getting a shot. It all depends, though, on what you do during the next few minutes.

Every whitetail hunter eventually jumps deer by mistake. Even confirmed stand sitters will see a white flag while on their way to, or from, an ambush. Some hunters deliberately jump deer to move them to other hunters. And hunters like me, who like to prowl for deer, one on one, *always* jump more than their share. It happens to me a lot—probably more than it should. Like most hunters, I kill more deer by sitting on a good stand and waiting for them to come to me. But I love moving through the woods, meeting the deer one on one. And most of the places I hunt lend themselves well to prowling, and prowling hunters jump deer.

Each year, I make it a point to get to Quebec's Anticosti Island, off the mouth of the St. Lawrence River. This 130-mile-long island has a population of more than 100,000 deer. Best of all, hunters are assigned exclusive zones, so there's no one else in the woods to mess up your hunt. Anticosti is an ideal laboratory for polishing your hunting techniques because you can jump dozens of deer in a single day and see how they react. Many of the tricks I've learned there have translated well to other hunts both at home in New England and across the country.

Too many hunters who have jumped a deer figure that they've blown their chances of ever seeing that deer again, so they just wander on, looking for other deer. Sometimes, especially in extensive northern woodlands with low deer densities, you may, indeed, have blown your only chance. There, without tracking snow, it may be hard to see your deer again. The buck may run a mile or more in essentially featureless terrain. In most areas, however, especially in smaller chunks of country where deer densities are high and territories are small, jumping a deer is no tragedy—if you're prepared.

Make Quick Decisions

There are no hard and fast rules about what to do when you jump a deer. Each situation is different, just as each hunter and each deer differ. But, once you see that white flag waving (and, believe me, it does not indicate surrender)—or the skulking shadow of a wise old buck slipping away with his tail clamped down to hide that flag—you have to make some quick decisions that often mean the difference between success and failure.

The time to begin making your decisions about what to do when you jump a deer is long before you ever see the flags flying. Before you even enter the woods, you have to ask yourself how well you know the terrain, yourself and the habits of local deer. Your response to a flying flag is likely to be very different if you've never seen the country before than if you've hunted the same 200 acres every season for a decade.

If you are hunting in unfamiliar country, get a topographical map of the area and study it before you hunt. Topo maps can indicate where you might find "funnels"—natural travel routes such as wooded draws between open fields, low saddles in steep ridges, dry crossings between a chain of beaver ponds—or " sanctuaries," such as impenetrable swamps and bogs. These are places that deer often head for when they're jumped.

Drive roads in the area to learn the lay of the land. If there's an airport nearby, a few dollars spent on a "sightseeing" flight is a great investment. Or, if there's a mountain in your intended hunting area, climbing it to look over the land is a wise move. Remember, the more information you have on the terrain you are hunting, the more likely you are to make the right decision when you jump a deer.

Another factor to consider before you ever see a deer is the weather. Deer behave one way when it's windy, another when it's still and a third when it's drizzling or pouring. Weather, of course, influences the hunting and hunter, too. If, for example, it's been dry and the leaves underfoot are crunchy, that will force you to make a different decision than you would make if everything was wet and quiet.

Finally, the hunter must assess his abilities. If you can move through the woods like smoke, have eyes like an eagle, and can snap an accurate shot off in a fraction of a second, you can make different choices than you can if you were born—as I was—with two large left feet, eyes that peer at the world through thick glasses and reflexes better suited to hitting standing targets than moving ones.

The ideal situation, of course, is to see the deer before he sees you, assess whether it's a deer you want, and then make your killing shot before he jumps. Unfortunately, that doesn't always happen. Deer blend well with their backgrounds, so if you're moving and they aren't, the chances increase that more deer will see you before you ever see them.

When your first indication of a buck is the sight of the south end of a northbound deer, your body inevitably reacts with a shot of adrenalin, and everything goes into high gear. Keeping your cool and making good decisions can make all the difference between having a diet of venison or beefsteak.

The first decision you have to make is if you should shoot. Sometimes, that decision is made for you. If your license is bucks-only, and you can't see antlers, obviously you can't shoot. Even, however, if you do see a legal deer, taking a running shot is a big risk.

My friend Gerry Lund is a skilled gunsmith from New Ipswich, New Hampshire. He's also a phenomenal rifle shot and is blessed with uncanny eyesight and reflexes. He can spot a deer and get off a killing shot—even through thick woods—while you or I would still be wondering what the fuss is all about. Gerry has no hesitation about taking running shots.

For most of us, however, slinging lead at a running deer is an invitation to a clean miss or, worse yet, a bad hit and a wounded deer. Unless you are offered an exceptional shot (such as the Nova Scotia spike that bounded broadside across a meadow 60 yards in front of me two years ago), my advice is to wait. A deer bounding through thick cover is a *very* tough shot; usually it's not worth the risk.

If your first look convinces you that this is either not a legal deer or one you don't want to shoot, tear your eyes away from it and start searching the woods around you. Deer often travel together. That waving white flag is designed to warn other deer and give them something to follow. When the deer are grouped and all bound away with flags flying, the peekaboo effect of a collective group of tails bounding among the trees also serves to distract predators, preventing them from singling out an animal and pulling it down. Don't let that happen to you.

Bucks seem to instinctively know that predators may be distracted by lots of flashing white tails. Several times, while the does and fawns of a group bounded away with tails held high, I've spotted bucks skulking in the opposite direction with their tails clamped down and no white showing. Usually, unless the deer were moving toward you when you met them, they will bound off more or less in the direction they were already headed. If there's a buck among the group, he'll frequently bring up the rear and will often retreat rather than follow the crowd. So, if you see a group of does and fawns, look behind and to the sides. You may see a buck and get a shot.

If the deer you jump is legal, but you can't get a shot off, keep track of where he goes. Jumped whitetails generally don't run far—when running they can't use their senses to detect danger ahead—and even a wise old buck will often stop at the first screen of cover. You are counting on the fact that most deer in a group don't know what—or where—the danger was. They'll stop sooner than a deer that knows why he's fleeing. If you are carrying an accurate, scoped rifle, be ready to take a rest and a shot when the flight stops.

While you're watching the deer, try to determine how severely he was spooked. If the buck is taking slow bounds, he may be nervous but not badly spooked. He is just putting a little space between himself and you. That's the deer most likely to stop and give you a shot. If, however, he moves low to the ground with several hard acceleration jumps before breaking into long, ground-eating bounds, then he is badly alarmed and will travel quite some distance before settling down again.

Some hunters have reported being able to stop a jumping deer with a grunt or snort call or even a loud whistle. Though I've been able to stop deer that other hunters have jumped toward me with these techniques, I've never been able to stop a deer I've jumped. In my experience, any noise from me only serves to accelerate the deer's exit. Calling may have a place in dealing with a jumped deer, but it comes later, not during the initial flight.

By now the deer is probably either already out of sight or has stopped to give you a shot. You've also had a chance to look around for other, hidden deer. If you don't have a shot, you have to decide— quickly—how you're going to play the next few minutes.

For me, the decision depends largely on the area's cover and terrain.

You have three options once the deer you've jumped is out of sight— you can pursue him, you can stay put and hope the deer will return, or you can forget about the deer and look for others.

The third option, forgetting about the deer, almost never makes sense. After all, you know precisely where he was. And, if you know the terrain at all, you should have some idea of where he might be going. That kind of information is valuable. Even if you didn't like his looks, bucks are actively seeking does throughout most hunting seasons, and by keeping track of the movements of does, fawns and yearlings, you can keep track of the buck's eventual location.

That leaves the other two options: move and stay. If the walking is quiet, and the terrain is reasonably open (allowing you some chance of seeing the deer), or if you will have the chance to ambush the deer at some point along their likely travel route, then moving makes sense. If, however, the walking is dry or frozen and noisy, or if you moved the deer out of a spot where they are likely to return, then staying put may be more productive.

If you are going to move, you must move quickly and decisively, which is why you need to be gathering information before you jump a deer. If, when the flags fly, you stop and think, "Where am I?" or "Where are the deer going?" you will probably miss your chance.

One of the most effective techniques for getting another look at a jumped deer is to slowly and quietly follow him. The best trailing route, however, is not directly on the buck's tracks; deer check their back-trails. You need to turn the tricks on the deer, staying just behind the first screen of cover where you can see him without him noticing you.

If you are going to trail the deer, and if the walking is quiet, the best time to begin moving is the instant you've concluded you will not get an immediate shot. Turn at right angles to the deer's flight path, preferably with the wind at your back and run (don't walk) about 50 yards as quickly as you can. Don't worry about the deer hearing you. Chances are either the deer is still moving, or he may think you are another deer crashing away from danger.

When you stop, pause quietly for a minute or two and look around.

Remember, there are deer in the area, and you just might see one. If you don't see any deer, begin stalking *slowly* on a path that parallels the deer. At this point, you have two distinct advantages: You know approximately where the deer is, while he still expects to see you where you were or on his backtrail; and deer that think they might be followed will often circle downwind to get a look at or whiff of the danger. If you are already downwind and moving with extra care, you might catch them at their own game. This only works, though, if you move with extreme caution, one step at a time, scanning the entire area between steps.

The other possible reason to make a move is to ambush the deer at some likely funnel ahead, or as he moves toward security cover, which you've found earlier. If you know of a possible ambush, it often pays to make your first move directly *away* from the deer. If the deer stop and hear you moving away, they'll often relax, mill around, then slow their pace as they proceed in their original direction of travel. That buys you time to make a circle to your ambush spot. This technique can work well whether the walking is quiet or not. The noisier the walking, however, the bigger you must make your circle.

There are times, however, when moving after you've jumped deer is precisely the wrong thing to do. When walking is noisy, when you are in a place that the deer are obviously using heavily, or when the deer you've jumped is young, curious and not badly spooked, or all three, you may be better off to sit tight and wait for his return. After all, the deer had a reason for being where you jumped him, and he may want to return.

I first tried this trick on Anticosti. For several days, when I jumped deer, I'd simply stay put and see what happened. About 50 percent of the time, those deer would make a circle and come back right to where they'd started. They acted as if I'd kept on moving after them, so they simply circled back to the place they wanted to be and watched their backtrail for danger.

Last year, during the antlered-deer-only phase of New Hampshire's three-week deer season, I put this information to work—again. Prowling through a hemlock swamp onto an oak-covered knoll, I jumped two bedded deer. Though I saw no more than a brief glimpse of flags, I got the sense that one was very small, the other only average-size.

The leaves were fairly dry, and walking was noisy, so I leaned against a tree and waited. Scanning the ground on the open knob, I noted many places where the leaves had been pawed by deer searching for the abundant acorns. There were also several obvious places where pressed-down leaves identified recent beds. The deer were hanging tight on this swamp-surrounded knob because it offered food, water and security all in one tiny area.

A half-hour after I'd jumped the deer, I heard a rustling in the swamp, and a doe and her fawn—a buck by the whorls of hair where his antlers would grow—eased back onto the oak knoll, ears swiveling, noses and eyes alert for danger. They ate a few acorns and bedded on the knoll. I watched them for more than an hour, hoping a legal buck would join them.

This time my strategy didn't provide venison, but in the same neighborhood a few years before, I'd taken a fine, fat little buck with my muzzleloader after I first jumped him and his companions off a similar oak knoll. Young deer are especially vulnerable to the sit-and-wait strategy, but even a wise old buck will come back to an area he considers secure.

How long do you wait? Naturally, it depends on the situation and its conditions. As I did on that oak knoll, use the time to look carefully around, first for other deer, second for deer sign. If there's little or no sign that deer are regularly using the area, stay only a short while. If, on the other hand, you get a sense that one or more deer are using that spot regularly, try, first, to determine why, and then judge whether it's worth waiting. Generally, I'll give the spot where I jumped a deer at least a half hour. I've seen nervous bucks stand still for 20 minutes without so much as flicking an ear.

If you're pretty sure that the deer you jumped was a buck, but conditions are too noisy to follow, try bringing him back to you. I've brought in curious yearlings on Anticosti by snorting back at them when they stopped to snort at me. I've never had a deer respond to a grunt call or to a bleat, but I see no reason why it wouldn't work.

You've got three factors working for you when you jump a deer and just stay put. Most important, there was a reason why that deer was in that spot. He may choose to come back. Another deer may be in the neighborhood for the same reason. Second, if you aren't moving, you aren't going to further spook the deer. Third, whitetails are naturally curious, and they will often risk coming back to see what spooked them if they weren't scared too badly.

Sometimes, too, it's possible to combine the techniques for dealing with a jumped deer. When there's quiet snow on the ground (a crust is worse than dry leaves for stalking), or the leaves are wet enough to allow tracking, I'll sometimes wait a half-hour or more at the site where I jumped the deer, then take the track and follow. The pause gives the deer a chance to calm down. I move quickly on the track as long as it moves in a fairly straight, purposeful line. When I see the traces beginning to wander, I slow down and, often, move 50 to 100 yards downwind before easing along toward where I suspect the deer may be.

During the waiting time, you can also consider where the deer was and where it was moving toward. That may point you toward a specific area to hunt.

Just remember, deer don't disappear after they run out of sight. They have to go somewhere. Remember, too, that deer are social creatures—especially during the rut—so one deer can often either lead you to, or attract, the deer you may be pursuing.

The next time you see those white flags flying, don't surrender. And don't curse out loud—you'll spook the deer. The hunt has just begun. ◈

From Outdoor Life, *November 1991*

'Tails from the Bedroom

by Michael Pearce

Forget the rut...a hunter's most dependable opportunity awakes when bucks slip off to sleep.

A S A GROUP, WHITETAIL HUNTERS are excited by what is easily seen. Show them a rub with the shine of a Louisville Slugger or an alfalfa field dimpled with tracks, and they'll salivate like a Pavlovian pooch.

Yet as tempting as it is to hunt breeding and feeding sign, these are not the most consistent setups; the rut is short-lived, and many mature bucks hit the feed fields only at night. Instead, it's often best to back off into cover and hunt a buck where he's most patternable— in his bedding area.

No doubt one reason many hunters ignore bedding areas is simply because they don't stand out like a field of corn littered with fresh droppings. The little nests of matted grass or flattened leaves are impossible to detect unless they're at your feet and, in places with vast habitat, can seem like proverbial needles in the haystack. But with a little deductive reasoning and an understanding of whitetail behavior, you'll be able to rule out at least 90 percent of that haystack.

Since a buck chooses a bedding area where it can detect danger, it also stands to reason that the bedding area offers an escape. One favored setup, for instance, has a buck bedded near a saddle between two ridges. That way, no matter where the danger comes from, the buck is just a bound away from safety, either going over the top of the ridge or down the ravine that leads to the saddle.

When searching for a potential bedding area, a buck is going to try to find his ultimate sanctuary, a veritable fortress that can be defended by eyes, ears and nose. Often, that means a perch on the edge of a bench or ridgeline where he can see danger approaching from below while a tailing wind warns him of threats from behind. Should the breeze do a 180°, the buck can simply switch over to the other side of the ridge. If it comes from a quartering angle, the deer may move to a slope facing another direction.

Of course, as with all hunting strategies, there are variables. Heavy hunting pressure may push deer farther and farther from food resources, so the closest likely bedding area is not necessarily the favored one to hunt. Many times pressured bucks will leave the woods altogether, taking sanctuary where hunters simply can't get at them...or in places where other hunters would never think of looking. Example: Several years ago, an Ohio hunter arrowed a 200-class typical as it slipped from it's bedding area, a five-acre cattail thicket bordered by Interstate 70 on one side and a housing development on the other. No doubt, literally thousands of hunters had driven by the spot on their way to the state's additional big woods.

There are several ways to determine exactly where an area's whitetails are bedded, the most obvious of which is to bumble through promising spots and look for the telltale white flashes of alarmed tails. It's a great technique...to find where deer used to bed. Whitetails, especially old bucks, pick a bedding area for its security, and many times if that security has been compromised bucks will abandon an area for weeks or months at a time.

During the season, the best way to find a hot bed is first to locate the predominant feeding area. Then, with the wind in your face, follow the trails upward, looking for major routes heading into potential bedding spots. When you find a trail that looks like a motocross track leading toward a brushy bench next to an escape ravine, chances are you've hit pay dirt.

The ultimate scouting technique is to wait until the season closes and then head afield with the first fresh snow. The entire travel/bedding area scenario will be laid out in brown and white and it makes no difference how many bucks you bounce from the area—they'll be calmed by next fall, and probably using the same bedding area. If you live in an area not blessed with snow, wait until the season closes and head afield after a good rain. The beds will be mashed down and tougher to spot, but the fresh tracks should lead you right to them.

As a general rule: The bigger the bed, the bigger the deer. While you're at it, keep an eye out for one or two huge beds tucked away from the others, possibly next to a brush pile or a mound of rocks with an easy escape route. Often they are the ones made by mature bucks that will be even bigger next fall.

Bedposts

As with in-season scouting, the number-one rule of hunting bedding areas is never, *never* to let a buck know you're around. Let him catch your scent one time and you can probably kiss him good-bye for weeks. This means that rather than set up right in the midst of the bedding area (where you're almost certain to be seen or scented as you come and go), stay to the outside and wait on major entrance and exit routes.

How close you set up depends on how the deer are moving. If it's early in the season and they're still traveling while it's light, you may be able to set up halfway between feeding and bedding areas. But if the pressure has been on and the bucks are mostly nocturnal, you may have to hunt right on the fringe, a ticklish proposition, to say the least. Thankfully, you can usually tell when it's not safe to get any closer: Brush and steep elevation changes are a sure sign of imminent beds, as are small meandering trails leading from the main path as the deer disperse to lie down.

Confronted with a good trail coming out of the bedding area, many hunters simply throw up a stand and start their stakeout. However, like hunting over rut or feeding sign, this is not always the best bet; mature bucks will usually shy away from easily traveled, major trails as they come and go from their sanctuary. Rather than amble the well-beaten path through mature hardwoods, a buck is more likely to follow a wrinkle in the terrain—like the edge of a ravine—that lets him use his eyes to cover one direction and his nose to cover another. When it comes time to hunt, consider all the variables in your area—routes bucks may take, major trails, travel patterns of the deer, etc.—and choose your wind direction and approach route carefully, making sure you don't spook animals as you come and go.

Four-Corner Bedding

One of the wonders of the American whitetail is its wide range of habits and habitats, a versatility that presents localized challenges for those who hunt them. To help pinpoint bedding areas in different parts of the country, we've enlisted four regional experts who can spot a potential bedroom almost as well as the bucks themselves.

NORTHEAST WOODLANDS: Jody Hugill, from State College, Penn., has a string of a dozen consecutive bucks by bow in the Appalachian Mountains. Since the majority of his bow season falls before the rut, he's a master at finding bedding areas. His first rule is to concentrate on the upper one-third of the mountain. His second is to worry more about topography than cover. "A lot of people say 'hunt the brush, that's where they bed.' But that's a heck of a problem because we may have miles of brush up on our mountains," says Hugill, a pro-staffer with Lohman Game Calls. "I set my stands almost entirely by the lay of the land. If a ridgeline is cut by a steep ravine it's a perfect place for a buck. Any abnormality, like a small rise, could also work."

Top Tip: "If the bucks are largely nocturnal, try calling from an afternoon stand that's within hearing distance of their bedding area," says Hugill. "Sometimes grunts or soft rattling will fool a buck into thinking other deer are already on the move, and get them up and going a little earlier."

SOUTHEAST CLEAR-CUTS: With a lifetime's experience of serious Dixie deer hunting, Bo Pitman knows where to find—and how to set up on—hot southern bedding areas. "They'll be in clear-cuts, either hardwood or pine, that are about three to eight years old," says Pitman, co-owner of White Oak Plantation in Tuskegee, Ala. "It's thick enough to offer protection, they're hidden and there's still plenty of browse to snack on. As long as you don't spook them out they'll just keep coming back...it's their home."

While some southern clear-cuts cover hundreds or even thousands of acres, Pitman concentrates on smaller areas and sets up where his hunters can get an open shot. "We have some of our best luck on 10- to 20-acre clear-cuts," says Pitman. "We'll set up on a logging road that goes through the brush, or better yet, where a strip of mature hardwoods sits between two clear-cuts. If you can play the wind right, you can catch them as they're coming or going, or maybe when they're just up and moving around. Good clear-cuts offer enough cover, so bucks don't mind getting up and moving around a bit."

Top Tip: "If you can ever get an overcast, drizzly sort of day with a prevailing wind, *hunt it*," says Pitman. "Those deer will often come later in the morning and go earlier in the afternoon. There's also a much better chance they'll get up and mill around during the middle of the day. It's a prime time to hunt near bedding areas."

MIDWEST POTPOURRI: A well-traveled whitetail expert based in Missouri, Brad Harris annually spends close to a hundred days afield. He's quick to point out the need to keep an open mind when looking for bedding areas, especially in America's Heartland. "The

Midwest offers such diversity—not just from state to state, but even from farm to farm," says Harris. "In some places the bucks will bed on traditional hardwood ridges. A few miles away they may use an overgrown pasture or a field of thick CRP grass. Or, they may bed in a thick fenceline where they can see danger coming for half a mile. You've got to do your homework and look for places where the odds seem to be especially in the buck's favor. And don't get too hung up on doe bedding areas. There are enough good places available that the big bucks will often separate from the does."

Top Tip: "It's always important to be versatile in the Midwest," says Harris. "If you find a good bedding area but there are no big trees, try a ground blind. If the deer are nocturnal and not moving at dawn and dusk, try setting up at the edge of the bedding area in the middle of the day. Chances are a buck won't stay in one bed all day. It'll probably get up, move around a bit, browse some and quite possibly give you a chance."

WIDE-OPEN WEST: The places where Gary Connor guides on the Great Plains look more like antelope or mule deer country than whitetail land. No wonder, then, that the bucks he hunts have developed similar traits. "It's not uncommon for the bucks we hunt to travel two miles between feeding and bedding areas," says Connor. "They can bed anywhere—CRP, river bottoms—but they really like the sand hills in the tall sage."

Connor keeps his hunting strategy as wide-open as the country he hunts. "Most of my hunts will have us on the highest point at first light," says Connor, whose Silver Mesa Safaris of Amarillo, Tex., boasts a 75 percent success rate on bucks averaging over 150 Boone and Crockett points. "We'll try to see them leaving their feeding area, figure out where they're going and move in to intercept them. Spot-and-stalk techniques let us stay away from the feeding and bedding areas themselves. If we think a buck went ahead and bedded before we could get to it, we'll watch that area that afternoon and try to get on it when it heads back to feed."

Top Tip: "These open-country whitetails can be pretty patternable—doing the same thing day after day as long as nobody disturbs them," says Connor. "But scout from a distance with good optics and don't move closer until the hunt. If they even see your truck in the area it could change their bedding habits 100 percent."

From Outdoor Life, *October 1997*

Playing the Field

by Michael Pearce

If you hunt crop-loving deer, know one thing: It's all in the approach.

◆

FOR DEER HUNTERS, FARM FIELDS are truly fields of dreams. These favored feeding grounds seduce whitetails into forsaking woodland security for succulent treats like alfalfa, high-protein beans and corn, and luscious grasses—temptations deer can't resist, even when they sense they are putting themselves at risk.

Although farmlands do indeed bring deer out into the open, hunting over them is far from live target practice. Anyone who has sat in a bean field knows that once a load of hot lead goes singing over their heads, whitetails change their dinner reservations to five minutes after shooting light.

Field hunting, especially for wary mature deer, is less a matter of waiting for them to step out of the woods than intercepting them on

the way to the field. It's called hunting the final approach. And the way to do it successfully starts with knowing when and where to set up your stand for ambush.

Early Fall

Your first priority during the early part of the season is to determine what crops deer are keying on. "When the bow season opens in

October, it's still pretty warm, life is easy, and the deer don't necessarily need high-protein food like corn," says Jody Hugill, a consultant for Lohman Game Calls.

"Instead, they're more likely to hit alfalfa. It's still green this time of year, and if it's been cut recently, it's really tender." Other early whitetail choices include clover, sprouting winter wheat, green soybean plants, and regional favorites like kudzu.

As for stand placement, Hugill begins scouting where many hunters end their stand search—at field edges. "It's almost always a mistake to put your stand right on the edge of a field," he says. "Most of the deer you'll see from there are does, and even they will stop coming out until after dark as the season progresses.

"I start at field edges and walk deer trails back into the cover, looking for intersections where two, three, or even four or more trails come together. That way I figure that I double—or quadruple—my odds."

Other good stand sites are near features that funnel deer movement, like sharp ridges, ditches, dense foliage, and "staging" areas where deer can wait for darkness near a field without being seen.

Hugill's observations have led him to theorize as to why bucks are even more of a challenge. "Once they've been pressured, bucks won't use the paths that does do," he says. "Those routes are too obvious. Instead, they'll travel where they can get out of sight in a hurry. The

EARLY-FALL STANDS should be placed 100 yards deep along approaches to favored pre-rut crops like alfalfa. Recommended sites: a) dense-foliage staging area; b) trail intersections; c) funnel (here, a creek and bluff); d) intersection 1/4 mile up main trail (morning stand).

lip of a steep valley, for example, is an ideal route. If they see or hear danger they bail off the lip and they're gone."

This means you should have several stand sites prepared in anticipation of variable wind directions, and scout different sites for morning and evening hunts. A buck may travel through the afternoon shadows to a staging area not far from a field, but he'll usually move past such areas well before daylight the following morning. Expect this movement and place your morning stands farther from fields than your evening stands.

Also keep in mind that as the season progresses, hunting pressure and thinning foliage cover make deer feel less secure. Stands should therefore be moved farther into the forest later in the season. During a recent Pennsylvania bow hunt with Hugill early in the fall, the opening-day stand from which I took a good whitetail sat barely 100 yards from the edge of an alfalfa field. Three weeks later Hugill took deer while hunting approach routes to that same field, but a quarter of a mile deeper into the woods.

The Rut

Once the rut begins, breeding exceeds feeding as a daily concern for bucks, and it is increasingly difficult to predict which crops they'll hit. Scout field edges at midday for tracks and droppings to determine which crops are the recent favorite with local whitetails. Your search may reveal something even more helpful: "Bucks often create scrapes near field edges," says Terry Rohm, a hunting consultant for game-scent manufacturers Wellington Outdoors. "Early in the rut, before bucks start chasing does in earnest, these scrapes are the places to set up."

Whitetail bucks also have a habit of making scrape lines along travel routes near ridges and brush lines far back into cover, especially where they can leave their calling card near several high-traffic deer trails. If you find such a place, set up there early in the rut.

When the rut begins to intensify, your focus should change, says Rohm. "Set up wherever the does are. Once you find where they're feeding, you'll find bucks. I've done well setting up off main trails leading to fields frequented by small groups of does. Given enough time, it's inevitable that the bucks will show up looking for them," he says.

Rohm concentrates on the downwind side of fields during the rut. "If

FIELD-HUNTING TACTICS during the rut are simple: Find fields where the does feed and you'll find bucks. Recommended sites: a) field-edge scrape (during early rut); b) scrape line farther into cover; c) main trail 100 yards into woods downwind of field.

the does are using the field regularly, it's not uncommon for bucks to circle the downwind side," he says. "They can stay hidden in the brush and still check for hot does with their noses."

Many hunters see the late season only as a chance to salvage an otherwise unsuccessful hunt year—they're willing to take the first deer, be it buck or doe, that comes along. But others have slightly different objectives.

"I love to hunt the late-season muzzleloader hunts," says Tony Knight, creator of the MK-85 modern muzzleloader. "Seems like the only bucks left are the real big boys. And if the weather is rough enough you can get one."

Whitetails often leave the rut weakened by weeks of single-minded pursuit of does. Now more mundane matters come to the fore—such as preparation to survive the coming winter. Suddenly there's a vigorous push by deer to put fat back on. That's why Knight says you should concentrate your efforts near secluded cornfields. "By the late season, the deer have been hunted for many weeks, so they're pretty goosey," he says. "They like out-of-the-way cornfields, cornfields with timber on at least three sides—something they can slip in and out of quickly."

To minimize detection in the usually sparse late-season cover, Knight sets up 50 to 75 yards on the downwind side of well-used trails

THE ART OF CORN STALKING

*I*F YOU HAVE A FIELD OF STANDING CORN ON YOUR HUNTING GROUNDS, CONSIDER YOURSELF BLESSED, MAYBE. CHANCES ARE YOU'VE FOUND WHERE DEER ARE FEEDING. THE QUESTION IS, CAN YOU SEE DEER—MUCH LESS GET A SHOT AT ONE—IN THIS TYPE OF COVER?

One method is to stillhunt across the rows of corn under windy conditions, heading into the wind and peeking down rows. The racket made by blowing cornstalks can cloak even a clumsy approach to a bedded deer. Another option is to drive the field with a line of hunters moving down the standing stalks to a group of standers.

If the field lies adjacent to a tract of heavily hunted land, try taking an opening-morning stand along a route where deer are likely to flee the hunting pressure for the safety of the stalks.

"I try to find a topographical feature like a point that juts in or out of a field leading from good cover," says Brad Harris, a call designer for Lohman Game Calls. "There's an excellent chance a place like that is a deer entrance or exit to the field." Other potential entry points lie where cornfields narrow and where they immediately lead to another field.

High stand placements are the norm in such spots–they're the only way to get a decent view down into the thick cover. But once you're set up, plan on staying for the whole day.

"Deer feel so secure in standing corn that they're more apt to rise at midday, stretch, move around, and perhaps even feed a little," says Harris. "If you're in the right spot, you may be able to take a good buck at high noon."

A LATE-SEASON HUNT should concentrate around secluded, high-protein cornfields, where deer fatten up for winter. Recommended sites: a) 100 yards into woods, 50 yards on downwind side of main trail; b) at field edge (only during harsh weather).

heading to cornfields. Weather conditions dictate how close he sets up to the field.

"If the weather's mild you have to back a ways off," Knight says. "But if it's really cold, especially when there's plenty of snow, the deer move earlier in the evening and feed a lot longer in the morning. If it's really bad I set up right at the edge of a field; when does stroll in, that's my cue to get ready—a buck is often right behind."

From Outdoor Life, *September 1995*

78

Stands That Deliver

by Gary Clancy

It's no secret that some stand sites are far more profitable than others. Selecting a super-stand site requires forethought, study and trial and error.

———◆———

MY FRIEND DALE CHELL OF Aberdeen, South Dakota, would rank in the better-than-average category of whitetail deer hunters. Although he frequently hunts in his adopted home state, for more than 40 years Dale has returned to a little hunting shack tucked in the timber of northwestern Wisconsin to spend the week of Thanksgiving hunting deer with friends and family.

Most years, Dale manages to put his tag on a buck. But this season while all Dale was seeing were does, a hunter from a nearby camp dropped seven bucks during the week, five of them on the first day of the season, and all seven were shot from the *same stand*.

Five hundred miles northwest of where Dale hunts, another friend, Bob Dahl, hunts in the wilderness country that forms the border between Minnesota and Canada. Climbing atop the same stand he has occupied for more seasons than he can remember, Bob chambers a round in his favorite deer rifle and sits back to wait for a buck to show. If you are in the mood for wagering on a long shot, you can bet that Bob *won't* come back into camp with a hefty North Country buck. The more than 50 bucks Bob has taken from his stand stack the odds in his favor.

And then there is the plywood platform strapped in the branches of a spindly pine just in from the edge of a good-size clear-cut; it's the stand my friends and I have come to call "Old Reliable." My long-time hunting partner, John Tidemann, selected the site for the stand eight years ago. Since then, the small group of friends who gather each year at John's cabin for the deer season have made certain that someone is always occupying Old Reliable. When someone in our group kills a buck from that well-used perch, he climbs down, and someone else takes his place. Most seasons, half of the bucks hanging from our camp game pole were killed by hunters posted atop that

3 x 3 sheet of plywood. On at least one occasion, every buck taken during the season fell to the bark of a rifle echoing from that nondescript pine. None of us can recall just how many bucks have tumbled within rifle shot of Old Reliable over the years.

Those are just three of the many super-stand sites I am familiar with, and I'll bet you know of places like these yourself. These are stands that just seem to provide deer year after year after year. Well, such consistent success has little to do with luck. The fickle and unpredictable rut is also not much of a factor in the success of these stands. And none of the three stands mentioned in the beginning of this article overlook the highly touted trails that deer travel between feeding areas and bedding sites. Rather, each of the three—and every other super-productive stand site I have ever known—is situated to take full advantage of deer movement dictated by hunting pressure.

Unless you are on private, leased or pay-to-hunt property where the number of hunters on the property can be strictly regulated, then hunting pressure is going to be the dominant factor determining when and where deer move.

When whitetails are disturbed by the presence of hunters the deer forget about eating, drinking and resting: they even postpone breeding and its associated rituals (what we call the rut), until they are satisfied that danger is no longer present. Whitetails do this in two ways: One, they stay put and let danger pass them by; and two, they move to a place where the danger is not a threat. The first option becomes increasingly difficult as the number of hunters escalates. During the first days of the season, most whitetails move to places that instinct or past experience tells them will be safe.

The best stand site is along the route these harried deer will use to move from pressured areas to safety zones. Along the length of that route will be one, sometimes, two locations for a super stand.

Locating the Route

The premise here is simple: The deer will move from those areas of dense hunter traffic to those areas that attract the fewest hunters.

Fortunately, deer hunters are pretty much alike wherever they hunt. Most of us think that we really get back into the boonies when we hunt, but studies show that most hunters will be found within a half-mile of their camps or vehicles. If you doubt the validity of these studies, I invite you to get into a small plane and fly over a public hunting area on the opening day of the deer season. What you will see is a distinct "line of orange" decorating the ridges nearest roads and camps. From the air it is also apparent that those hunters who do penetrate deeper into the timber most often take advantage of the easy walking provided by logging trails, power line and pipeline rights-of-way and railroad tracks. It is further apparent that these hunters stay on, or very near, the avenues they used to arrive at their locations. The rest of the terrain will be void of hunters or, at best, harbor only a smattering of orange. Those are the places deer go when pressure puts them on the move.

An airplane survey is the best way I know of to quickly pinpoint the areas that receive the most and the least amounts of hunting pressure. The route deer will use to move from pressured areas to safety are also easily recognized from the air. Most of us, however, will not fly over our hunting grounds, especially when it must be done during hunting season to be most beneficial. Instead, boot leather and experience will provide the basis for our strategy.

In farm country, fringe-land habitat and river bottoms—the choices open to a whitetail attempting to get from one place to another—are limited. A deer spooked out of one woodlot that is connected to another by a brushy fenceline will predictably follow that fenceline. Likewise, deer following creek and river bottoms stick tight to the cover the timber affords.

In the big-timber areas of whitetail domain, the process of determining the route or routes used by deer that are on the move due to hunting pressure is not so simple. The often spouted advice, "Hunt the edges: that's where deer travel," is sound counsel indeed, providing that there is some sort of edge for deer to use as they make good their escape. The edges of big woods, however, tend to be scattered and erratic to a degree that often causes deer to ignore the edge in favor of a more direct route, making detours only when confronted with crossing wide-open spaces.

Most clear-cuts, by the way, do not fall under the category of wide-open spaces. Only the most recent cuts and then only those free of tops and slashing lack enough cover to make whitetails feel at home. To the hunter's eye, accustomed to appraising whitetail habitats by degrees of thickness, clear-cuts—even maturing ones—appear to constitute wide-open spaces. From a whitetail's point of view, however, a clear-cut, with its assortment of brush, slashing and new growth, is cover aplenty.

Even though bucks do not hesitate to cross clear-cuts, expect them to take the route that offers the most cover and to make use of any islands of concealment along the way. And that brings us to the next part of the selection process.

Your Super-Stand Site

In some cases pressured bucks have no choice but to exit along escape avenues that are so narrow that a stand placed anywhere along their length will do the trick. Hedgerows, treelines, fencelines, skinny creek bottoms and drainage ditches are all examples of meager escape passages that are easily covered. Selecting the site for a super stand becomes a challenge when the deer have the whole side of a mountain to use or a seemingly endless stretch of forest at their disposal. Then narrowing down the options that meet the criteria for super-stand sites becomes a matter of ferreting out every funnel along the route. A funnel is any feature of the land, man-made or natural, that restricts the deer's lateral movement.

The most easily recognized funnel is the "hourglass." Picture an hourglass in your mind and then relate that shape to your hunting territory. One wide end of the hourglass is the pressured area. The other, the end into which the deer trickle, is the whitetails' safety zone. You are looking for the "waist" in the hourglass; that is where you want to erect your super stand.

Most hourglass funnels are not formed by a manicured forest, but rather from characteristics within the timber. An example is the super stand of a friend of mine who hunts the sprawling hardwood valleys of the upper Mississippi River.

The section of valley Jack hunts is three miles wide by four miles long and is located between two roads. Jack built his stand nearly dead center in that 3 x 4 section. That alone would probably be enough to ensure that pressure from all sides would put a deer in Jack's sights. But Jack isn't interested in just filling his tag: he hunts big bucks, and the numerous mounts decorating his office and den are testimony to his success. Most of those big bucks have been taken from that one stand. Jack's stand is in the perfect bottleneck location: in an ancient maple on a 50-yard-wide flat area that lies between a nearly vertical limestone outcropping and a cold, deep trout stream.

Don't, however, expect every funnel to be so obvious. Remember Old Reliable, the stand on the edge of the clear-cut. It overlooks a funnel through which pressured whitetails flow just as assuredly as sand drips through the hourglass, but even the most imaginative mind would have difficulty conjuring up visions of that classic bottleneck at this location.

Instead, Old Reliable earned its name because John did his homework. He first determined where the most intense hunting pressure originated, and then he went looking for the stand's site. What he found was that hunting pressure was the heaviest on the far side of the big clear-cut where a well traveled logging road provided easy access. Another area with heavy pressure was a section of low-lying timber bordering a small creek that twisted through the forest a mile north of where John eventually put the stand. The site that John keyed on was at the opposite end of the clear-cut from the logging road, where a long finger of aspens protruded into the clearing and intersected a gentle ridge that ran the length of the clear-cut.

Then John hunted from several stand sites before determining that the attraction of the area was the spear of aspens. Deer naturally traveled the ridge when crossing the clear-cut and invariably dropped down into the welcome cover of the aspens. Any deer pushed out of the creek bottom by hunters would also eventually meander out of that tangle of aspens if hunter traffic was sufficient. Finally, John settled on the little clump of leftover pines on the ridge crest as the permanent location for his super stand.

The trial and error process that John went through before choosing the right location for the stand is par for the course. Last season I located what I think will eventually earn a reputation as a super-stand site. I know where hunting pressure originates, I have determined where the deer scoot for cover when the action heats up, and I have found the route they use to evacuate the pressured turf. Along that route is a narrow gash in the timber that has recently been logged over. Skirting the gap would mean a one-mile detour for any deer following the escape route. There are two locations, though, one on each end of the gap, where the deer only need to be exposed for 75 yards between protruding jags of timber.

Last season I placed my portable stand on the edge of the timber just south of the most southern of the two crossings, and 13 deer crossed that slash in the two days I hunted there. Only one made the crossing within point-blank range. A dozen deer slipped across at the distant narrows. Although this past year I did manage to drop a buck with a long shot as he picked his way across that skinny gap in the forest, for next year, an already-trimmed pine that overlooks the crossing is just waiting for my super stand.

Trophy Time

Although a super stand is the place to be whenever hunter traffic is sufficient to have deer on the move, if it's a big boy you're after, don't dilly-dally over that second cup of coffee in the morning. Big bucks will be moving before many hunters have moved at all. A buck that is large enough to sport impressive head gear is also old enough to remember previous hunting seasons. Although spikes and forkhorns may mill around and be confused by all of the activity, a big buck knows what all of the commotion means, and he also knows what he has to do to avoid it.

Having gone through all of the effort of finding a super site, I make absolutely certain that I am on that stand a full half-hour before shooting light. Most of the big bucks that friends and I have taken from super stands have been taken *early*. Hunting from Old Reliable, for example, has nearly always resulted in a downed buck during the first hour of the season. Last year, John's son dropped his first buck from the stand when the season had only been open for seven minutes. The single shot from his Uncle Tim's .270, which took the hefty eight-pointer, was the first shot of the morning. The season before, I had the honors on opening morning. Even though day was nothing more than a ragged scar of pink on the eastern horizon, I was ready when the 200-pound 9-pointer came sneaking along the ridge. When he turned to drop downhill and intercept the aspens, I sent a 117-grain Federal Premium boattail through his lungs.

Super stands are only super when hunter traffic is sufficient to prod the deer. After opening weekend's activity, there often is not enough action to make sitting on a super stand worthwhile. In Wisconsin, for instance, where I hunt each season, and where the season is traditionally held during Thanksgiving week, the opening weekend is great for occupying a super stand. From Monday through Wednesday, though, the woods are quiet, transforming super stands into superduds. I spend those days hunting from alternate stands or stillhunting in places where I can take advantage of the natural movements of deer. On Thanksgiving Day, however, a good share of Wisconsin's 1 million member army of orange will be back in the woods, trying to fill unused tags. Pressure will remain sufficient through the close of the season on Sunday to make a super stand, well, just *super*.

From Outdoor Life, September 1990

Bucks on the Front Lines

by Gary Clancy

"Weather" you like it or not, hunters who are out and about when a storm's moving may just be enjoying their best chances to take a good buck.

◆

REMEMBER THE SUMMER WHEN Hurricane Gilbert was chewing up chunks of Mexico and churning toward the Texas coastline? Remember the scenes on the evening news that showed long lines of people standing at grocery store check-out counters, their carts laden with such staples as canned meat and bottled water? Well, obviously those people knew that the storm was coming. They knew that they might not be getting out again to get groceries for awhile, and they were laying in a supply of provisions to see them through the tough times ahead.

The birds and animals we hunt react similarly in the face of an approaching storm. Instinctively, everything from bobwhite quail to bull elk know when a storm is on its way. Without supermarkets to rely on for a cache of food, however, these birds and animals instead gorge themselves prior to the arrival of the bad weather. That is why one of my favorite times to hunt whitetails is when a storm has been forecast. Hunters who know where the deer will be feeding and who can arrange to be there when a dramatic change in the weather is imminent often experience the best hunting of their lives.

The first part of the puzzle, discovering where the deer are feeding, is up to you. I can tell you this much—animals do not switch feeding sites in the face of a storm. They know that when the need to fill their tanks is urgent, that is not the time to be shopping around for a new spread. If you know that the whitetails have been scarfing up acorns along a certain ridge of white oaks, for example, then that is the place where you want to concentrate your hunting efforts when a storm front is approaching.

And don't worry about the time of day, either. Animals that normally feed only at twilight will be up and around at midday if a storm is bearing down. Even the big bucks, those that have evolved into nearly nocturnal creatures, will succumb to the urgency of the moment.

The second part of the puzzle—knowing when to be afield—is as simple as flipping the switch on your television. Nearly every local television station now gives its viewers a "satellite picture" of current and expected weather conditions. When that satellite picture indicates a storm front moving into your area, try your darndest to arrange your schedule so that you can be in the field just prior to the arrival of the bad weather.

If you have access to cable TV, you don't have to wait for the evening weather report. During the hunting season, I spend a few minutes each day watching "The Weather Channel" as the forecasters walk me through the current weather conditions, the immediate forecast and the long-range outlook. Many times I have rearranged my schedule to take advantage of the fronts indicated by the pretty lady with the pointer. Contrary to all of the jokes and banter, I have found these forecasts to be reliable a good share of the time.

Of course, while actually at deer camp, most of us do not have access to a television, but we can still pick up the weather on the local radio station, or better yet, invest in an inexpensive weather radio. These handy units will constantly give you the forecast for your area, forecasts that are upgraded hourly by the National Weather Service.

Take the time to watch the television for a few minutes, or listen to the radio. Forecasters can indicate the most productive times for hunting.

Last December, during my state's late bowhunting season for deer, the forecaster on "The Weather Channel" warned viewers that the first major winter storm of the season was building up strength and heading in from across the Rockies. The storm, which according to the forecaster would bring substantial amounts of snow and send temperatures plummeting, was due to arrive in my hunting area on Wednesday evening. I made the necessary arrangements and was in the woods by noon on Wednesday.

I put my stand in a clump of birch where I could overlook the intersection of three trails. The trails, all showing signs of frequent use, snaked down from the south-facing slope above, an area that I knew was laced with brush-choked ravines and was a favored bedding area for deer at that time of the year. After merging beneath my stand in the birch clump, the three trails became a single path leading down through a sumac thicket and emerging at the grassy edge of a strip-picked cornfield. I knew that the cornfield was being used by several dozen deer each night, but that steady hunting pressure along the trails leading to the corn had resulted in most of the deer postponing their trip until darkness had forced the hunters from their stands. I hoped that the approaching storm would cause the deer to abandon their nocturnal habits and make the trek to the cornfield while shooting light remained.

My hunch was right. I had been in the portable stand for only an hour when the first deer, a string of five does and fawns, came down the hill and past my stand. An hour later three more does made the trip; then a short time after that two more. By 4 P.M. there were two dozen deer feeding in the tattered cornstalks, but still no buck had shown. The first wind-driven snowflakes slapped me in the face. Somewhere in the leaden skies above, a flock of whistling swans, their voices it has always seemed to me mourning the end of autumn, made their way south. When I looked back at the cornfield, there was nothing but a sheer wall of swirling white. The storm had arrived.

A spike buck came slipping down the trail, moving with the quick steps that his kind make when they are anxious to fill their bellies. I had been holding out for a good buck, and had passed up several spikes earlier in season, but now time was running out. By the time I settled the argument going on inside of me and decided to take the shot, the spike was gone, just melting out of sight into that ever constricting sheet of white. Kicking myself, I tried to see through the snow, watching up the trail the spike had used and ready now should another buck show.

One did, but this boy was having nothing to do with the well-packed trails used by the other deer. Hard to my left I caught a shadowy blur of gray motion, but the longer I stared at the spot, the more I became convinced that what I thought I had seen had been only a figment of my imagination.

Then just as I was ready to turn my watery gaze back to the main trail, the buck took another step—a drifting, silent, shadowy form floating in a world of swirling white. Like the spike, the big buck was hungry, but unlike the spike, this veteran was too smart to rush. He took things one step at a time. Stopping, he thrust his nose to the swirling wind and cocked his ears as he tried to sort out the danger sounds from the hissing whine of wind strumming naked branches. All I could do was stand on my platform and eyeball the buck. The big deer was plenty close for a shot, but there was no way that I could make the turn, lean out around the birch and draw on the buck without him detecting me. My only hope was that he would work his way around my position and give me a shot as he quartered away.

Then the buck did just that, passing directly downwind of my stand. He was close enough to the base of the birch that my scent, scattered as it was by the strong wind, blew over his back. I knew then that I was going to get my chance, and my right leg began to dance as it always does when a close-range encounter with a big whitetail draws to its conclusion. I made my turn on my heels. The buck stood in a clump of gray dogwood 15 yards away, his black nose up into the wind, his broad back dusted with falling snow, his heavy, nut-brown rack with 10 or 11 or 12 points angling back over his neck. I forced myself to forget about the rack and to concentrate on the opening six feet ahead of where the buck stood. When the buck lowered his head and took a step, I drew the old recurve. A black nose, a white-ringed eye and a mass of antlers filled the opening. One more step and I released.

The shot looked good; I can yet see that yellow fletching flying true to the mark. But at the last moment something went wrong. Probably the big buck squatted at the sound of the string. Maybe I held at full draw a tad too long and had just shot high. Maybe the arrow ticked a slender shoot of dogwood. I don't know. I do know that I watched as the arrow sliced air just over the buck's snow-flecked back and that quicker than I can tell it, the buck was gone, leaving me shaking and limp with disappointment.

I missed that buck, but I know that I would never have seen him if not for the storm forcing him to move while shooting light remained.

For several seasons after, I hunted without success during stormy periods. My mistake was that I wrongly assumed that the deer would be looking for the same thing that I was when the weather turned nasty: comfort. I tucked my stands into the quiet little draws and pockets where the wind lost its bite. I hunted the lee side of ridges and the downwind edges of evergreens and cedar swamps. And I saw very few deer.

A whitetail couldn't care less about comfort when it comes to chowing down in the face of an approaching storm. After a buck has filled his tank and settled down to ride out the storm in his bed, yes, then he will search out the quiet places where the wind will not suck the heat from his body. But when hunting the storm fronts, forget about being comfortable. The deer will feed in their accustomed places, regardless.

Once while hunting the big-timber country of northwestern Wisconsin, where deer are not as plentiful as in some areas of that deer-rich state and hunting pressure is far less intense, I found myself at midweek of the rifle season virtually alone in the woods. Without the rut or other hunters to encourage deer to move, I was spending long uneventful hours on stand and trying unsuccessfully to stillhunt over dry, noisy forest litter. At noon one day I was sitting in the truck eating my lunch and listening to the radio when the announcer warned of a major winter storm moving rapidly across Lake Superior. Due to smack into my area by late evening, the storm was to bring strong winds pushing up to a foot of new snow and temperatures that would plunge below zero by dawn. I gulped down the last of my sandwich, shouldered a portable stand, grabbed my Ruger and struck off into the timber. There was a quickness to my step that I had not felt for a few days; call it anticipation.

I knew where I wanted to be. There was a clear-cut of maybe 100 acres a half-mile down an old logging road. The seedlings that had been planted by the timber company had grown to shoulder height. Those pines and the ever present scrub oaks gave the deer plenty of cover in the clear-cut, and the area was a favored feeding site, as well. On the northwestern corner of the clear-cut, a long tentacle of wrist-thick aspens snaked out of the dark timber into the relative open of the cut. Those aspens afforded the whitetails a natural travel lane from the timber to the chow line. A cluster of fence-post-thick pines decorated a mild slope just above the finger of aspens. I had hunted here before, and now put the portable into the pine that I had trimmed the previous season.

When the hump-nosed doe and her two fat fawns slipped out of the aspens and into the stubby pines of the clear-cut, I forgot about the cold. I glanced at my watch. It was 2 P.M. The approaching storm had the deer up and feeding early all right, now if I could just tough it out until a buck let his belly drag him from his bed to the clear-cut.

The doe and fawns fed slowly up to my stand and then moved off behind me. Soon after, a flicker of gray in the aspens caught my attention. Then there was another slight movement, and through the 8x42 binoculars I found the deer, both bucks—the first a forkhorn, the other larger. There was a yard-wide trail dissecting the finger of aspens, a trail that I had helped nurture over the years with a little judicious pruning of young shoots. When the forkhorn stepped into the slot, I put the crosshairs on his chest and waited for the other buck to make his move. The forkhorn stepped out of the frame and the bigger, one, a nine-pointer, took his place. When he lifted his right front leg to step over a fallen aspen, I sent a 117-grain Federal Premium through his lungs.

By the time I had taken pictures, dressed the buck and dragged him back to the truck, the wind was carrying the first of the foot of snow that would fall during the night.

After the Storm

If you can't get out before the storm arrives, try to be in the woods when the weather breaks. Deer that have weathered the storm will be hungry when everything has passed, and midday feeding is not uncommon at this time. The longer the storm lasts, the more pronounced the post-storm feeding binge will be.

Like other ruminants, the whitetail has four sections to its stomach and, of course, is a cud chewer. According to Leonard Lee Rue III's excellent book *The Deer of North America*, "There is a lapse of 14 to 18 hours from the time a deer's food is eaten until it has been passed up again as cud, chewed, reswallowed and passed through the reticulum." My observations have convinced me that a deer becomes most anxious to feed once the cud-chewing process has been completed. The whitetails that I have observed that have missed a feeding period but still have a cud to work over appear content in their beds. Animals that have been holed-up long enough to have passed the cud-chewing stage are antsy and anxious. If you have a storm severe enough to force deer to stay put for longer than 24 hours, you are reaching the point at which the stomach of a whitetail will be completely empty.

Several years ago, my brother-in-law and I were hunting a northern state during a December muzzleloader season. A blizzard struck with force on the second day of the season, dumping two feet of snow in 12 hours and sending the temperature plunging to minus 27°. For two days after the storm the temperature remained in the minus 20° range. Although we hunted hard on both days, the only deer we saw were those that we pushed from their beds; the only tracks were those of the deer that we had disturbed.

But on the second night after the storm, the intense cold mellowed. When we rolled out of our sleeping bags in the black of predawn, the old thermometer hanging on the door of the pickup camper registered a balmy 1°. We wolfed down our breakfasts, pulled on gaiters over heavy felt pacs, took the cold rifles from the cab of the truck and waded into the timber.

Deer tracks were everywhere. Shadowy forms moved off silently on our flanks. Larry and I parted company on the point of an outcropping. He dropped into the bottoms to hunt near a cornfield; I headed for a stand of white oaks on a distant ridge.

My tattered log book shows that I saw 27 deer that morning before the block-bodied buck made the mistake of pawing down through two feet of snow for an acorn within range of my stand. Larry saw nearly as many deer feeding in the corn. It seemed that every deer in the woods was up and feeding that morning. And, oh yes, we never encountered another hunter.

It takes a little something special in the way of dedication to stick it out in the face of an approaching storm, or to venture out in a storm's wake. Our instincts tell us to stay home where it's warm and comfortable. I am not advocating taking chances that could be life threatening. Once you see the number of deer that are active just before and again after a storm, that discomfort will seem a small price to pay. ◈

From Outdoor Life, *November 1990*

Push-Over Deer Drives

by Gary Clancy

It doesn't take a military strategist to plan a
successful deer drive. All you need are a small
group of hunters, the right terrain and deer that
can be coaxed into moving.

O VER THE YEARS, I'VE READ dozens of articles that have gone into detail on how and where to conduct drives for whitetail deer. Some of these stories have been complete with diagrams indicating the positions of drivers, posters and deer. A few of the "blueprints for whitetail action" that I've seen would confuse Gen. Norman Schwarzkopf.

Most of these military-like maneuvers designed to outwit the whitetail deer are a total flop. Complicated drives usually result in confused and disoriented (a nice way of saying lost) drivers, posters left to wonder what happened to the rest of the crew and deer that must be snickering just a bit as they watch the circus unfold.

So what do I offer you? Yep, another article on deer drives complete with diagrams on how they should work. The difference is that the four drives I'm going to discuss are simple. These drives work with small groups, consisting of two to four hunters. There are no complicated maneuvers, which only serve to confuse party members and make the drive ineffective from the start. These are the drives that my friends and I use when we drive deer.

But a discussion of specific drive plans is worthless without a basic understanding of why drives succeed and why they fail. We need to look at three points: when to drive, where to drive, and how to get posters and drivers into position without alerting every deer in the drive area. Once you have these three points down pat, you can use the four drive plans that I've included in this article—or drives of your own concoction—to help you and your hunting partners get your sights on more deer.

When to Drive

Drives are the answer when deer are not moving naturally or being forced to move because of hunting pressure. If there are other hunters in the woods, you are better off sitting on a good stand and letting them push deer past your position. Likewise, it is a good idea to stay on stand during those times when deer are typically moving about, namely during the early morning and late-afternoon feeding periods and all day long when the rut is in progress.

Weather is also a factor to consider. When it is very windy, deer are reluctant to move because they know that all of their senses will be impaired. Wind scatters scent, creates a racket in the woods and is constantly whipping brush and leaves into motion. This leaves deer feeling vulnerable as their senses of sight, smell and hearing are greatly handicapped. Under such conditions, most deer will be tucked deep in heavy cover waiting for the wind to die down.

Whitetails are extremely nervous when the wind is howling, and instead of sneaking out of cover ahead of drivers, they will frequently burst forth at full speed and will remain on the move when they go by the posters. Shots at stationary deer are rare on drives conducted during windy weather.

Unseasonably warm weather during the hunting season also will greatly decrease natural deer movement. Once a whitetail is all decked out in that gray winter coat, the animal doesn't handle heat very well. When the temperature rises, deer will seek shaded areas and simply bed down, moving mostly at night until the hot spell breaks. Because being out and about in very warm weather is uncomfortable for hunters, too, many choose to hunt only a short time in the morning and perhaps an hour in the evening. The absence of other hunters in the woods means that you cannot depend upon deer being disturbed and sent past your stand. Stillhunting, too, is a poor choice in hot weather because the footing is usually dry and crunchy, making it nearly impossible to sneak undetected within range of a deer.

All this combines to make driving your best choice in hot weather. But be forewarned: Driving is hard work, and hot weather quickly saps the energy and enthusiasm from most hunters. When driving

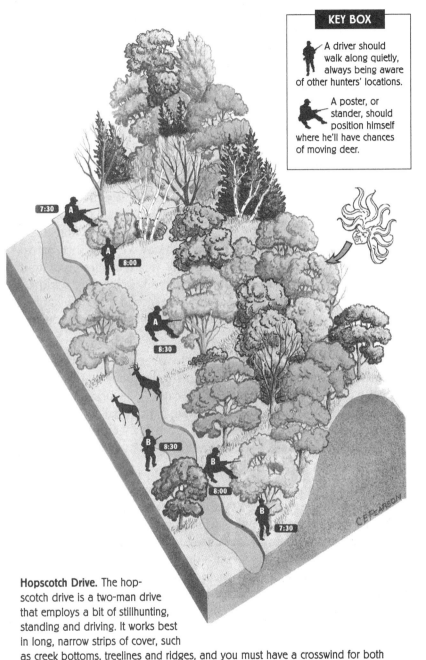

KEY BOX

A driver should walk along quietly, always being aware of other hunters' locations.

A poster, or stander, should position himself where he'll have chances of moving deer.

7:30 A

A 8:00

A 8:30

B 8:30

B 8:00

B 7:30

C.F.PEARSON

Hopscotch Drive. The hopscotch drive is a two-man drive that employs a bit of stillhunting, standing and driving. It works best in long, narrow strips of cover, such as creek bottoms, treelines and ridges, and you must have a crosswind for both hunters. The drive works like this. Pick the area to hunt, and the two of you start at opposite ends. Beginning on the hour, Hunter A hunts slowly in the direction of Hunter B for a half-hour. Hunter B sits while Hunter A is moving, and then moves while Hunter A sits. On short drives, we may alternate moving and sitting every 15 minutes.

deer in the heat, plan short drives, take long breaks between drives and make sure that there is plenty of cold water available. Even with all of these precautions, chances of seeing a lot of deer during hot weather—even on a finely executed drive in super cover—are slim. This is because whitetails are so reluctant to expend energy when it's hot that they're much more likely to hold tight and let drivers pass by. A hunt in southeastern Ohio last fall provides the perfect example.

The rugged hill country of this corner of the state is home to good numbers of deer, as well as some real bruiser bucks. On the eve of the firearms deer season opener, a small group of us had gathered at the farm home of our friend John Weiss, whose articles frequently appear in the pages of *Outdoor Life*. Despite what it said on the calendar, a record-shattering heat wave made it feel more like a Fourth of July celebration than a deer camp. The next day we found that natural deer movement was being limited to the first few minutes of light in the morning. And as the heat persisted, hunting pressure couldn't even be counted on to move the deer by the second day. It quickly became obvious that if we wanted to find whitetails, we were going to have to go in after them.

Weiss, his son, Mike, and their friend, Al Wolter, were all intimately familiar with the area we were hunting. Together they mapped out strategies for drives through prime deer cover. We worked hard, but moved few deer—the norm when hunting in hot weather. Deer are simply so reluctant to move during hot weather that no matter how well the drive is planned, you are going to walk by more deer than you put on the move.

Cold weather, on the other hand, is the catalyst for more drives than hot weather. This is evidenced by the fact that drives are the norm for hunters in the North Country, where sitting all day on a stand can be pure torture when temperatures dip down into the single digits. The normal procedure is for each hunter in the group to hunt from a morning stand and then meet back at a predetermined site at midmorning. Drives are conducted until midafternoon, when once again the hunters split up to take their evening stands.

Where to Drive

The most common recommendation you'll hear is to drive the heaviest cover available. This is sound advice if the deer have been subjected to significant hunting pressure or if the wind is howling. And, yes, you can argue that the best cover in any area will always hold some deer. But don't believe for a minute that pounding through the thickest available cover is always the best tactic. Many times I have run into situations that have made driving open timber, or what I like to call secondary thickets (those places that don't look really "whitetailish" to the hunter), a better bet. Let me explain.

In Wisconsin a few years ago I ran into a typical midweek situation. There were few hunters in the woods, and the deer were feeding relatively undisturbed on an abundant acorn crop. Deer that are keying on acorns and are not being bothered have a tendency to bed down at the food source, rather than making the trip to thicker bedding cover. Proof came when we switched from unproductive swamp drives to pushes through open hardwoods—we had deer running all over the place.

A similar condition exists during the whitetail rut. When a buck has procreation of the species first and foremost on his mind, he spends as little time as possible holed up in heavy cover. Once hunting pressure slackens, you can bet that bucks will be on the prowl looking for receptive does. And because family units of does frequent more-open terrain, that is where I like to conduct drives during this time of year.

Another thing that I've discovered is that no matter where I've hunted, from Minnesota to Mississippi, bucks in hill country have a habit of bedding down near the tops of ridges. And why not? After all, there they can rest comfortably (if a whitetail ever does) while thermals bring them messages from below, and their high vantage point lets them spot hunters from quite a distance. As a result, my brother-in-law and I have learned to key in on ridges when making two-man deer-hunting drives.

There has been so much written about a whitetail's penchant for heavy cover that in many areas today the best deer cover is liberally sprinkled with orange coats. Drives should never be conducted through cover in which other hunters are hunting. And this is where my "secondary thickets" come into play. These are the places that most hunters overlook as they search for the best deer cover. These are also the places deer seek out when they find their favorite haunts crawling with hunters.

When I first began to hunt deer, it was with a shotgun in a slug-only zone in southern Minnesota. That part of Minnesota, like much of the Midwest, was comprised mainly of corn and soybean fields. Once these fields were harvested, deer concentrated in the few remaining woodlots and skinny river bottoms. This was also where most hunters focused their efforts. My friends and I, however, avoided these hard-hunted, obvious whitetail strongholds and spent our time driving places the other hunters overlooked—namely, small wet sloughs seemingly better suited for pheasants and mallards. Many of these sloughs had no trees at all, though some had a few straggly willows or cottonwoods. These sloughs ranged in size from 20 acres down to about the size of a three-bedroom rambler. And not only did we always fill our tags while driving these secondary thickets, but we took some very large, corn-fed bucks in the process.

Two-man Ridge Drive. As I mentioned earlier, deer tend to bed down just over the crest of a ridge. The two-man ridge drive is designed to take advantage of this fact, and again it is a combination of tactics—this time stillhunting and driving. Hunter A takes the left side of a ridge, Hunter B the right. Each hunter moves slowly along his side of the ridge as if he were stillhunting. Bucks disturbed by one hunter will often cross over the crest of the ridge and drop down the other side—affording the other hunter a shot. A great way to stay in contact with each other without alerting deer is to use mouth diaphragm turkey calls (or crow calls if there is a fall turkey season in progress). A few clucks or caws every few minutes is all it takes to ensure that you and your partner stay in line.

I've witnessed the same thing happen where clear-cutting is a common means of harvesting timber. Hunters tend to concentrate their drive efforts in the thicker conifers and hardwoods while ignoring the more open clear-cuts. Where slashing has been left behind and new growth has begun to sprout, clear-cuts provide super cover for whitetail deer. Don't overlook them when planning a potentially successful deer drive.

Positioning Drivers and Posters

Most deer drives are doomed before they ever get started. The reason is that posters alert deer while moving into position or drivers get antsy and begin the drives too soon.

The secret is to have posters sneak quietly into position well before the drive is scheduled to begin, then make sure that none of the drivers approach the starting line until the agreed-upon time. Some of the most effective drives that I have been involved in were those in which the posters simply remained on their morning stands and at a predetermined time the drivers assembled for the push.

Two hunters can easily work out the details of a two-man drive between themselves, but drives involving three or more hunters need a "drive captain." The drive captain should be intimately familiar with the area being driven. It is his responsibility to position the posters, assemble the drivers, ensure that the area to be driven is free of other hunters, and signal the beginning and end of the drive. Drives involving a number of hunters who do not elect a drive captain are often a joke. Most of the time is spent standing around the tailgates of pickup trucks while everyone draws meaningless lines in the dirt with sharp sticks and argues about where and how to make the next push.

Don't bite off more than you can chew, either. Drives are most effective in small blocks or narrow lanes of cover. I've seen groups try to drive an area the size of the Adirondacks with a half-dozen hunters. It typically doesn't work.

Because most drives are set up so that deer are pushed into or across an opening, taking up a post position right on the edge of the opening is mighty tempting. The problem with this is that deer tend to run across openings. You will get better shots at stationary or slow-moving deer if you post 50 yards or so deep in the cover. What happens is that when a whitetail is faced with the problem of crossing an

Three-man Ravine Drive.
Don't ask me why, but no matter where I hunt I find that deer love to bed down in those ravines and fingers that jut out from main valleys and extend into fields or clear-cuts. Ravines are perfectly suited for three men to drive, although two can get the job done if the single driver does a lot of zigzagging. The poster should position himself 50 to 100 yards in from the tip of the ravine to ensure shots at deer moving slowly before the animal breaks over the top.

opening, it nearly always hesitates as if it were trying to make up it's mind about whether or not to really dash across. That is when you will get your best opportunity to shoot.

There are still some hunters who believe that the more noise they make the more deer they will move. These groups come screaming through the woods at a half-run, hollering, banging on tin pots and, in some cases, shooting in the air to get deer on the move. You would think they were trying to get a bunch of lazy, half-dead Holsteins on their feet. For every deer that these noisy gangs see, you can bet that a dozen more slipped out undetected as soon as the racket began. It is far more effective to have drivers walk along naturally and within sight of each other. This way deer will not be running scared when

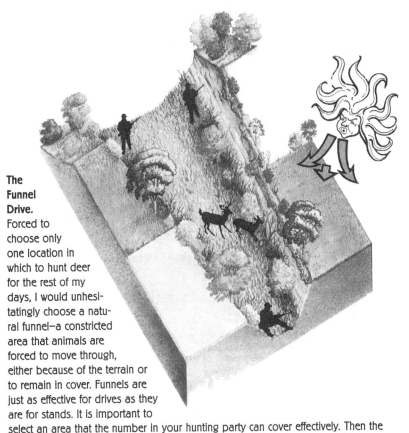

The Funnel Drive. Forced to choose only one location in which to hunt deer for the rest of my days, I would unhesitatingly choose a natural funnel—a constricted area that animals are forced to move through, either because of the terrain or to remain in cover. Funnels are just as effective for drives as they are for stands. It is important to select an area that the number in your hunting party can cover effectively. Then the idea is to position posters where the funnel necks down and drive the cover toward the posters. Deer will funnel through the constriction naturally, and the posters will often be afforded shots at walking or standing animals. Funnels naturally occur in river and creek bottoms, but they abound in other settings as well.

they go past the posters, but instead will simply be picking their way along allowing plenty of time for good clean shots.

Drives have a bad (and undeserved) reputation for being dangerous. One simple rule eliminates the possibility of someone getting shot on a drive: Drivers never fire toward posters, and posters never fire in the direction of drivers.

Feel free to experiment with the drives described and illustrated here. Drive plans are like good recipes—they can be made even better by adding just a pinch of this and a half-teaspoon of that. But remember, simple is the key to successful drives. ◈

From Outdoor Life, *October 1992*

103

In Thick with Deer

by James E. Churchill

One man has bagged 12 bucks from the same stand. You won't try to get them out but will literally join them.

I WAS STANDING AT THE FOOT OF the swamp knoll when it became light enough to see. Voles scampered from one clump of moss to another, and a chickadee roosting on a black ash tree limb slowly turned its head from side to side as if trying to decide whether it was really morning.

Then I heard him coming and every nerve tightened. It wasn't the steady sound that a deer makes when coming out of a swamp in the late afternoon, but the stop-and-go sounds of a deer heading for his day bed. Suddenly, his dark back appeared above the bearberry shrubs. He was too close. I knew he would see me when I drew but I drew anyway, and the shaft scraped softly across the bow. My shoulder joints popped in protest as they were suddenly loaded with 80 pounds of string weight. If the buck saw or heard it he didn't react.

The shot was true and his rack now hangs in my garage with a dozen other large bucks I have collected with a bow. But I will never forget the careless way this deer moved. He was relaxed, off guard, and as much at ease as a whitetail deer ever gets. Conversely, when I had seen him on the uplands a week or so before, he was like a tightly wound spring, paranoid and vigilant. He obviously had never seen a hunter in this thick swamp and didn't ever expect to see one. He almost completely let down his guard.

That was the first buck, but since then in gun and bow seasons over a 16-year period, my son and I have taken 14 bucks from that exact location. All were taken near a certain knoll in a deep swamp. This proves to me that there are certain small areas that bucks favor for bedding grounds, especially when the weather turns cold and hunting pressure is heavy. Further, when one buck is taken another will take his place in a year or two.

Most of the long-time hunters in this area have such a place that they return to year after year to get their buck. One man I know has bagged 12 bucks from the same stand, and they all were heavy-racked deer with eight and 12 points. Another never fails to get his deer on the first or second day from his favorite swamp stand. I investigated these locations and they look a lot like ours.

From our stand you can't see more than 30 feet except down the shooting lanes we have cut. There are no deer trails. Even in the snow, a few tracks leading in would be all you could find. But look very carefully and you will see deer beds and an unusual collection of deer pellets. The significance of this will be explained later.

The layout could have been purposely designed by a wary old buck to provide an unapproachable hideout. First, it has a dense stand of balsam and spruce trees stunted by the cold marsh soil so that they grow short and thick. This cuts the visibility to a few feet in most areas. You couldn't see a deer if you happened to walk through except for the first jump or two.

It is also protected by a dense growth of shrubs such as bearberry and willow. Overlaying the shrubs are blown-down trees and dense alder stands. It is impossible for man or animal to go through this barrier without telegraphing his presence far ahead. I have even heard snowshoe hares running through this cover. A deer sounds like a man and a man like an elephant. Bucks don't sleep very soundly in the daytime, if they actually sleep at all, but even if they did, the sounds would wake them.

This cover superbly protects the deer, but the best long-distance warning is created by the tall aspen and pine that grow along its edges so that the swamp forms a corridor. This corridor is almost perfectly aligned east and west. The wind in this part of the world usually blows from the west, southwest or northwest. Thus, it is usually funneled down the corridor, bringing with it all of the messages that a breeze can tell a buck.

An easterly wind is just as effective, of course, but even during the few times that the wind blows directly from the north or south it will tumble over the tall trees lining the swamp on either side and be borne down to ground level, where it will then fan out in both westerly and easterly directions. Only on calm days does man have a chance of fooling the deer completely. But even then he has to be standing in the swamp before the deer gets there or else it will hear or see him coming.

This almost impenetrable fortress also offers food and water to the buck. Water is available in numerous puddles and rivulets flowing through the swamp. By the time it freezes hard, snow has fallen and the deer can eat snow to quench their thirst.

Food is also in good supply. Deer will eat almost any kind of browse or grass in a pinch, but this location offers preferred foods. A few cedar trees were blown over or have low-growing limbs so that cedar needles are within reach of the deer. A deer can live quite well with only cedar needles for food if it has to. But along the southern bank of the swamp, red maple shoots grow in a thick stand. Patches of wintergreen, aspen, sphagnum moss and dewberry vines also are easy to find around the deer's bedding grounds. He literally could live out his days without coming out of his hiding place if that's what he wanted.

The bucks do come out for food, and it is no wonder. Ringing the swamp is a wide upland area that has grown up to ferns, new aspen shoots and several species of grasses. Several large red oak trees are scattered through the territory and they produce a good crop of acorns every three to four years. One huge beech tree also offers up a good crop of beechnuts in favorable years.

There is little doubt that this location is more comfortable. The considerable canopy of evergreen limbs keeps the air temperature higher here than in the open areas by retaining some of the radiated ground temperature. Further, it reduces the velocity of the wind so that the chill factor is less than in more open areas.

I originally found this buck's favorite bedroom by chance, but most everyone can find a place like this of their own if they are willing to put in the time and effort. Experienced deer hunters should study their hunting grounds very carefully, particularly in regard to swamps bordered by large expanses of highland. Probably at least one location will have the accommodations mentioned, maybe several will. But probably only a few will be particularly attractive.

Beginners or veteran hunters going to a new spot to hunt can start to zero in on a buck's hideout by talking to area department of natural resources employees, experienced local hunters or clerks in sport shops. Sooner or later a particular place will be mentioned time and time again as being a good place for big bucks. This will usually be followed by the statement, "But that's rough country. The bucks will head for the swamps the minute the shooting starts. A company of Green Berets couldn't get them out again."

You won't try to get them out. You will literally join them. Study "topo" maps to find a place that from the air looks like a square mile or so of upland territory with a swamp somewhere near the center. Mark all such locations on your map and start scouting. If the swamp has considerable deer sign entering or leaving, it is a favorable sign. This doesn't actually mean that it will be a hotspot. In fact, most big-buck hotspots won't be too clearly defined by tracks. Big bucks don't like other deer. They attract the predators. Except during the rut, they would rather be by themselves.

This bedding location is not the "core area" that has been mentioned many times in literature, but it can be identified by some of the same signs. Before the rut there may be a "licking branch" nearby. This licking branch is a sign that deer use a scent post to leave their sign. They are hard to find but are usually a maple or other hardwood branch that hangs over a deer trail. The dominant buck will lick the branches and most every deer that goes by that branch will smell it. By this sign, they will know that the dominant buck is still in the area. When he is killed, a subordinate buck will move in and take over his bedding grounds, which makes these choice locations productive year after year.

When the rut starts, the buck will likely make a scrape line nearby. Scrapes, of course, can typically be positively identified because of the broken branch tip hanging above it. The deer will lick and chew this.

If few hunters are about, the buck may sleep on the uplands. He won't be too far from his hideout, however, and should patrol through once in a while for this reason.

Before they come into estrus, does will frequently hide from over-eager bucks. They sulk in thick cover and the bucks soon learn to go into the swamps looking for them. Therefore, the buck might come by his bedding grounds as he looks for does.

After the rut, the buck will be tired and gun hunting season will open. The woods will fill with hunters and the buck will home in on his favorite bedding ground like a fox chased by hounds. Although it might have been difficult to find this area earlier, tracks in the snow should divulge his hangout now. I rely heavily on finding and analyzing the beds and droppings, whether on snow or not.

A big-buck bed, of course, will be big. No mistaking the size of his bed for a yearling or even an average-size-doe bed. He will usually bed down for about two or three hours, get up and move about a bit and then lie down again. He may or may not lie down in exactly the same place the second time.

A well-fed buck will probably defecate a dozen times during the day and almost always when he first stands up after bedding for a long time. By studying the location of the droppings, the hunter can often find where the deer commonly beds even if the signs of the bed have disappeared.

A large buck commonly has large droppings, so the number and size of the droppings indicate the size of the deer and the amount of use a deer is giving to a certain area.

If you are not successful in finding the buck's favorite bedding grounds before or during the deer season, keep looking after the season closes. The buck will probably stay around this preferred bedding ground for weeks after the season has ended. By that time, it will be so well-marked that it will be easy to find.

The next year, if that buck is still alive, he will likely use it again. Only if he is chased out three or four times during a short period of time will he abandon the hideout permanently.

After you have found a big buck's preferred bedding grounds, try to do all of your set-up work in one trip. Cut out shooting lanes if necessary but don't change the cover too much. A large amount of cutting and altering might spook the deer into leaving the location permanently.

You will probably have to hunt from a ground blind. A tree blind will be hard to find in most of these areas and, even if a large enough tree can be located overlooking the hunting territory, the cover will be too thick to see the ground. Usually very little altering needs to be done to make a ground blind. Just stand behind a short thick evergreen tree or inside a pile of blown-over tree trunks.

Your entry trail must be marked with care. You will likely be coming in to hunt before daylight in the morning because that is about the only time you can catch him out of his fortress. There is nothing wrong with marking the trail with small reflectors that will reflect the light from your flashlight so that you can walk directly to the stand with as little commotion as possible. Just remember to remove the reflectors when you finish hunting.

Try not to walk across the buck's trail when you go into the stand. He might pick up the odor from your tracks and be warned. Try to determine where he will come from and stand downwind if there is any moving air. Avoid wearing any type of scent at all. You don't want him to be interested in your exact location even if it is an attractor scent. When you see him coming you will have to move slightly to shoot, and if he is looking directly at you this might give enough warning to spoil the shot.

Bowhunters need a clear area for the arrow's flight, and it should connect to a portion of the trail that will reveal the entire deer, if possible. This will cut down on the possibility that a branch or shrub will deflect the arrow. No special equipment is needed by the gun hunter. A shotgun and slugs or buckshot will work just fine. I use my scope-sighted rifle because I am used to it. A scope gathers light and makes an accurate shot more likely in the dim light of the early morning. Also, if the deer stops in thick cover you can often determine parts of his body through the scope better than with an open sight. I use 180-grain, softpoint bullets in my .308.

Hunting deer in the swamps is an excellent way to get lost if you don't use some precautions. When there is a snow cover, of course, you can backtrack yourself out. But it is surprising how few people do that. Instead, they try to get out by walking farther and faster, often in the wrong direction. Always carry a compass for this type of hunting. Know the general direction in which you would have to walk to get out. If you forget your compass and the sun isn't shining, listen for traffic or, after dark, for signal shots. Walk in a straight line by lining up a tree or other landmark. Walk directly to it and then line up another and so on until you get out. If you can't hear anything, you can still walk out of most areas in an hour or two by walking in a straight line as explained.

Try hunting the swamps this fall. You might find a location that will provide point-blank shots at wall-hanging bucks for the rest of your days. ◆

From Outdoor Life, October 1990

Racks in the Rain

by Robert Willis

If you think that when the skies open up it's time to head for the cabin, you're all wet. Not only does buck activity increase when it rains, but so do your chances for success.

◆

WHAT IS THE WORD ON DEER hunting in the rain? For as long as I can recall, older hunters and outdoor writers have been preaching the same gospel when it comes to hunting deer in the rain: Namely, that hunting is good and deer are active in a drizzle, but that deer seek thick cover and remain inactive during hard showers, and that all hunters with an IQ above 10 do the same. Well, if you will forgive my pun, that advice is all wet.

I have spent enough rainy days in the woods to convince myself of three givens when it comes to hunting deer in the rain. The first is that deer do not suffer any discomfort in the rain. The second is that deer are almost always active on rainy days. And the third is that hunters who stay in camp when it's raining are missing the boat.

One of the problems is that we hunters tend to judge an animal's comfort zones by our own. If we are cold, we assume the deer are cold. If we are wet and miserable, we wrongly assume that the deer are also wet and miserable. But nature doesn't work that way. The nervous system of a whitetail deer is not like our own. Deer are not programmed to seek "comfort." Instead, deer adapt to changing weather conditions and go on about their business. If they didn't, and simply sought protection from the elements every time it rained, snowed or got too warm, they would quickly starve to death.

I say that deer are almost always active on rainy days because there are conditions that can accompany rain that will definitely cause deer to severely curtail all movement. Wind is the most common culprit.

Whitetail deer depend most upon their senses of sight, smell and hearing to survive. Wind interferes with all three senses, making it difficult for deer to detect danger, and thus transforming an already high-strung creature into a real basket case. It doesn't make any difference whether the wind is accompanied by rain or not; deer will move as little as possible during strong winds.

I cannot say how deer react to violent thunderstorms. The reason for this is that during 30 years of tromping around the places where deer live, I've seen a couple of hundred trees that have been struck by lightning. Any force that can split a sturdy oak from crown to trunk has my respect, and when forks of lightning begin stabbing at the ridges, I get out of the woods.

I am tempted to climb out on a literary limb and proclaim that in my

estimation, deer are more active on rainy days than they are on days when it is not raining. Indeed, my hunter's log, in which I record all of the pertinent facts of each day's hunt, including the hours hunted and number of deer sighted, backs up that claim. But I have a hunch that the reason why I see more deer per hour hunted on rainy days is not solely because the deer are more active, but rather because of my preferred hunting style on rainy days. Conditions for stillhunting are never better than when it is raining. An excellent example of how productive this wet-weather technique can be was a recent hunt that I enjoyed.

Sometime before the alarm clock rang, I had awakened to the sound of water pouring off the roof of our comfortable cottage at Callaway Gardens in west-central Georgia. I wasn't surprised. It had rained most of the previous day, and had still been coming down hard when we had called it a night. By the time the coffee was ready, I had my game plan for the morning figured out. I planned to sit on stand for the first hour of the morning, and then, just as soon as it was light enough to see well, I'd make my way to a particular long, narrow ridge where the previous afternoon I'd found a dozen whitetails— including two bucks that I'd elected to pass up—busy feeding on a bumper crop of acorns and hickory nuts. I was betting that the deer would be in the same pattern the following morning.

My host, Bill Jordan, wrestled the Suburban down a slick, Georgia-red-clay two-track and dropped me off in the bottom of a hollow.

"I'll pick you up here at 11:30," Bill said as I slid out the door. "Good luck, now."

It never does get full-light on rainy days. It seems to me that daylight just sort of oozes out of the wet blackness, and then you suddenly realize that it's as bright as it's going to get. That particular morning, I had been on stand less than an hour when I came to the realization that it wasn't going to get any lighter. I climbed down from the stand, removed the sling from my rifle—as is my habit when still-hunting—and began the long climb to the top of the ridge.

Near the crest of the ridge I spotted movement. Through my binoculars, I could see that what I originally thought was a doe was really a spike. I waited for the little buck to feed over the crest, then continued my slow ascent.

Conditions were ideal. The rain was coming straight down—heavy at times, then letting up to little more than a drizzle at others. Occasionally, patches of misty fog drifted over the rolling Georgia hills, cutting visibility down to a few yards.

Two hours later I came to a place where a saddle of loblolly pine cut through the hardwood ridge. Bill had erected a ladder stand at the edge formed by the pines and hardwoods, and I stood beneath the platform for long minutes using the binoculars to pry into the dark recesses of the thick stand of trees. A flicker of white caught my attention, and I trained the glasses on the location where I had seen the movement. Again I saw the flash of white, and this time recognized it as the upturned tail of a deer. For 20 minutes I stood under the stand and searched for more movement, but there was none. The deer, I was sure, had moved out of the pines and into the hardwoods on the far side of the saddle. I knew that if the other deer were feeding where I expected them to be, I would be close when I crested the ridge. So, to be as quiet as possible, I took off my rain gear and proceeded at a crawl—literally.

Fifteen minutes later I was on my hands and knees covering the last few yards to gain a view of the north slope of the hardwoods. As the slope came into sight, I dropped to my belly and scanned the bleak forest before me. Nothing moved. I reached inside my jacket and pulled out the binoculars. Eighty yards away a doe stepped from a clump of brush and began to feed up the slope. Three more does followed, then a five-point buck and another doe. Feeding slowly, as deer tend to do in the rain, it took the herd a half-hour to drop over the far side of the ridge and out of sight. I stood up slowly, stretching cramped muscles and debating whether to move on or stay put for a while. A hunch told me to sit tight. I'm glad I did.

A few minutes later a doe followed by a very respectable eight-point buck exited a little draw at the bottom of the slope and began to slowly feed uphill. I put the scope on the buck and studied him carefully. Slightly wider than his ears, the buck's light-colored rack sported short brow tines, but had long, curved, symmetrical main tines. My mind raced back a week to a hunt in another state when I would have given a week's pay to have seen such a buck. I don't consider myself a trophy hunter, but Bill Jordan had convinced me that the property we were hunting held some real monster bucks. To back up his claim he had shown me a dozen mounts of bucks he had taken from these same hills during the past 10 years. From the 163-point B&C typical down to the "smallest" 10-pointer, they were all beautiful bucks. And the buck that I was scoping was one that in another year would fit in that category. I elected not to take him.

Suddenly the buck and doe both turned and stood staring intently down the hill in the direction from which they had come. When the eight-pointer tucked his tail between his legs and hunch-backed his way slowly up the ridge—a sure sign that a buck higher up in the pecking order was approaching—I knew that I had made the right decision.

Slowly, I wiped both lenses of my scope free of rain and snuggled into the stock while at the same time peering over the top of the scope in the direction that the eight-pointer had been staring. A doe showed first, and then behind her I caught the first show of butter-yellow antlers against the backdrop of wet, black timber. I didn't have to look twice at the heavy nine-point rack to know that this was the buck I had traveled 1,500 miles south to find. When the big bruiser stepped into the clear behind the doe, I touched the trigger of the .25-06 and the buck crumpled.

Without the rain, which allowed me to quietly sneak into position on that hardwood ridge, I'm convinced that I never would have seen that buck.

A word of caution about stillhunting in the rain. Many hunters tend to move much too fast when attempting to stillhunt on rainy days. A quick pace is tempting, of course, because of the ease with which you can move silently through damp cover, but though you will certainly be rewarded with a look at more country, I guarantee that you will also be looking at far fewer deer than will the hunter who proceeds slowly. When stillhunting in the rain, I make a conscious effort to move at the same snail's pace that I use when hunting under less ideal conditions. Although it is true that you can move quickly without making alarming sounds when it is raining, whitetail deer are so well-adapted for motion perception that you will rarely escape visual detection when hurrying the hunt.

There are three reasons why hunters who venture out in the rain will so often find deer actively feeding during the hours we normally associate with daytime bedding periods.

The first—and the most important reason—can be attributed to the type of weather that so often follows a rainy period during the fall of the year. I am speaking of a cold front. Very often when the rain tapers off, it is followed by plenty of wind, a wind-direction switch to the northwest and high blue skies. Whitetail deer have an excellent internal weather forecasting system that rarely fails them. Because wind, more than any other weather condition, prevents deer from feeding on schedule, whitetails tend to chow down during the rain so that they can go into the windy, cold-front period with a full belly.

The second reason why there is often an increase in deer activity on rainy days is because there is a lack of hunting pressure on such days. Simply put: Most hunters don't like to hunt in the rain. Whitetail deer are quick to react to the respite from human intrusion and slip back into their normal routines, which include periods of feeding in late morning and early afternoon.

Yet a third reason why hunters will find deer feeding during rainy periods can be traced to the whitetail's well-documented penchant for being most active during periods of poor light. Under normal conditions this translates into active periods occurring around dusk and dawn. But when it's raining, skies never totally brighten. Deer are comfortable and relaxed under these conditions because their specially structured eyes allow them to see splendidly under what we humans would term poor visibility conditions.

I should also mention that your chances of finding deer feeding at midday in the rain increase in direct proportion to the availablity of preferred whitetail fodder at that particular time. For example, in my home stomping grounds of southeastern Minnesota, the deer depend heavily on the acorns of the red and especially the white oak. The best midday hunting in the rain occurs during those years when there is a poor mast crop. It simply takes a deer longer to get its fill in years when acorns do not litter the ground.

From what I've seen, rain does not interfere with a buck's main objective in life: namely, propagation of the species. I have never seen any indication that soggy skies have dampened a buck's enthusiasm for sex. And because it is the doe—and not the buck—that determines when the breeding actually takes place, it is probably safe to assume that nature has not instilled in the female of the species any anti-estrus switch that is tripped by moisture. When a doe enters that 24-hour period during which she is capable of conceiving, you can bet that a buck will try to find her, rain or shine!

On the same morning that I took the big nine-pointer in Georgia, Bill Jordan was occupying a stand overlooking a string of scrapes. The rut was winding down, but Bill had spied a huge 10-point buck working the scrapes earlier in the week, and he was determined to get a shot at the big deer. His determination paid off on that dripping, dreary morning when the big boy came chasing a doe within just a few yards of where Bill was perched. Unfortunately, when Bill tried to get his crosshairs on the moving buck, he discovered that his scope had fogged up during the wet morning vigil. The buck disappeared into the drenched timber, hot on the doe's tail.

The most miserable day I have ever spent in the rain while deer hunting is also vivid testimony that precipitation does not interfere with the rut.

It was mid-november in a northern state, and though it should have been snowing in earnest, it was instead pouring down rain mixed with sloppy flakes of snow and occasional barrages of sleet. I must admit that I thought twice about getting out of bed that morning, but I had drawn a coveted bowhunting permit to hunt a restricted state area with a reputation for harboring some real buster bucks. I had seen a couple of dandy whitetails during the first three days of the hunt, but had been unable to get a shot. That miserable day was my last chance.

I put my portable stand up in the spreading branches of a twisted maple tree on the southwestern corner of a rectangular-shaped, 40-acre chunk of extremely thick second-growth timber. Most of the buck activity I had witnessed during the previous three days had seemed to be centered around that parcel of woods.

This was back a few years, before I had splurged on a set of quality raingear, and by the time it got light enough to make out individual trees in the woods, I could already feel the cold dampness around my shoulders and neck. By 9 A.M. I had not seen a deer, and I was ready to call it quits, but as so often happens at such times, it was then that a buck made his appearance. He was herding a reluctant doe out of the dark timber and into the belly-high grass on the edge of the woods, and at more than 300 pounds with a neck so swollen that his head appeared too small for the rest of his frame, that buck was absolutely magnificent. Just before the doe completed her circle in the grass and took the buck back into the timber, I got the glasses on him. I heard myself suck wind as the rack came into focus through the rain-splattered lenses. All thoughts of abandoning the stand vanished.

Twice more throughout the long vigil in that maple I saw the huge buck. Once the same doe, or perhaps another, brought him out into the grass where the pair had circled earlier, and again in midafternoon the buck appeared with a small herd of does and fawns on the edge of the timber. When a smaller buck approached, the big boy lowered his head, laid back his ears and uttered a low, guttural grunt, causing the subordinate eight-pointer to duck quickly back into the woods. Each time the big boy showed I hoped that a doe would lead him closer to my tree, but he never came closer than a tantalizing 80 yards before melting back into the timber.

Throughout the day I fought the urge to climb down from the tree and try to sneak in on the buck, even though I was sure that I could move quietly enough. I also knew from having scouted the woods thoroughly before the season that my chances of getting an arrow through the thick underbrush were near zero. I hunkered deeper into the ineffective raingear, shivering uncontrollably, my only thought just to hold out for the last hour and hope for one last opportunity at the giant buck.

My chance came while the rain pounded down during the last minutes of shooting light. One minute I was staring at an empty field of sopping wet grass, and the next I was watching the buck shaking the water from his heavy coat like my Lab does after retrieving a duck. I didn't notice the doe at first, as she blended in well with the wet grass, and the rain and hour made it difficult to see. When I did pick her out, my heart jumped to my throat and my hand moved slowly for the bow hanging on a broken limb. The doe was walking my way. Surely, the buck would follow.

He did, quickly catching up with the doe and falling into step just behind her, his black nose only inches from her tail. Through the monotonous drone of falling rain, I could hear him grunt with nearly every step. Eighty yards, 60, 50, and the doe stayed right on line. My numb fingers tightened on the arrow nock. At 40 yards the doe stopped and the buck stepped up alongside her. I don't know what he whispered in her ear, but she must not have cared for the idea. She squirted away from the buck, not running flat out, but prancing in that easy manner with which whitetails cover ground in a hurry. In an instant the buck was on her trail. When he passed at 30 yards I made my draw and released.

Maybe the long vigil in the cold rain had made it impossible for my muscles to function smoothly when the moment came. Maybe my half-frozen fingers had caused me to make a sloppy release. Maybe the restrictive raingear had interfered. Maybe I had had a touch of buck fever. The arrow wasn't even close.

No, I didn't get that buck. But I see him often. All I have to do is close my eyes on a rainy day in the woods and there he is. That buck, and a lot more like him, is what keeps me out there looking for racks in the rain.

From Outdoor Life, *October 1990*

In Deep

by Gary Clancy

Problem solving for hunters who like to get into the thick of things.

T HERE'S NO BETTER EXAMPLE OF whitetail "escape" cover than a cat-tail marsh. But hunting these reedy, mucky jungles is so tough, few hunters properly exploit them—if they hunt them at all.

There's more to tackling these sanctuaries than conducting the common raucous brush-busting drive through the reeds. Start by locating plots with potential. Look for isolated marshes. The farther removed they are from other deer hideouts, such as dense woods or standing corn, the more deer become dependent on them. Size is important too. Large expanses of cattail marsh are next to impossible to drive effectively. Deer seem to know this, and when given a choice they invariably seek out the largest (read safest) marsh. If two wetlands are in close proximity, your best bet is almost always the one that covers the most territory.

Some areas of a marsh are better than others. Just like you, deer don't enjoy having their feet wet for too long. They like high-ground trails and slightly elevated "islands" or hummocks that allow them to get out of the mud and water. Old abandoned farm roads and logging trails also provide havens in the wetland. Look for plants that prefer higher ground than cattails such as phragmites (ditch reeds), willows, slough grass, and cottonwood trees. Locating these dry-ground sanctuaries can ease the task of scouting.

Regularly patrolled by bucks searching for does during the rut, these trails through the predominant cover make excellent locations to set up for calling and rattling. Don't just come stomping up the trail, though. It's important to access these openings from the "back door." The best way to approach is by a small boat or canoe. If this isn't possible, wear hipboots or waders and be prepared to go out of your way to avoid exposing yourself at the trail head or crossing a deer path.

Hunting cattails can be demanding to the point of masochism, but just getting into the thick stuff is most of the battle. Take the tips below to heart. They'll come in handy in cattails and anywhere else deer make their escape.

10 Tips That Make Dense Sense

THE BIG PICTURE. Whenever you hunt, the less accessible the land is by motorized transportation, the better. Where to start? Get a bird's-eye view. Aerial photographs are the best way to get a handle on an area's accessibility and are usually available through state or federal wildlife departments. Many hunters, however, find topographic maps easier to read. They are available from commercial outlets and from the Forest Service.

MAP ATTACK. One rule of thumb is that deer hunters don't like to venture far from their vehicles. Highlight on your map all territory within a quarter mile of any vehicle access points to the land you hunt, including trails accessible by ATV. This band is the area of highest hunter density. Now highlight in another shade everything between a quarter and a half mile on either side of the roads and trails. This area is subject to less intense hunting pressure but is probably hunted hard enough to send the largest bucks into escape cover. Your big bucks are in the heaviest cover within the unshaded portion of the map.

TAKE THE HIGH ROAD. In hilly or mountainous terrain bucks spend their daylight hours on the top third of ridges and mountainsides. They may travel the low country at night to eat and chase the ladies, but at first light they hustle their way to high ground. And it doesn't take a mountain to make high ground. A gentle ridge running through lowlands or a hogback jutting into a cedar swamp can attract bucks. If you're unfamiliar with the hunting area, a topo map is invaluable for pinpointing such features.

"Deer, like humans, will take the easy route whenever possible," says Jody Hugill, a respected deer hunter and game caller who hails from central Pennsylvania. "They make use of depressions, dips, saddles, hollows—any land feature that allows them to get where they are going quickly while expending the least effort."

TWO CARDINAL SINS. "Most hunters make one of two mistakes," Hugill says. "First, they get excited by the amount of buck sign they find in the low country and decide that the place to hunt is down low. What they don't realize is that the bucks that made all those scrapes and rubs in the flat fields did it at night. By shooting light those bucks are climbing back up to the thickets on top. Second, hunters try to pick a location where they have a panoramic view. They want to be able to see deer coming from a distance and have plenty of time to get ready for a shot. All this is fine if you want to just see a lot of deer, but the really big boys are rarely caught off guard in such semi-open areas. Hunting should be done down in the thick stuff—it should be darn near claustrophobic."

STAND TALL. In most cases a tree stand is the best way to hunt a thicket because it affords a vantage point over the tangles. As a back-up, take a ground blind on the edge of the heaviest cover rather than attempt to hunt it on foot. Position your tree stand before the hunt so that you can slip into it with a minimum of commotion. And because you should be picking your way to your stand in the dark, mark the trail in with glow-in-the-dark tacks or ties.

DAWN PATROL. Be at your stand site an hour before first light. The biggest bucks are most likely to make their appearance in the half-light of dawn, but hunting pressure or the rut can increase daytime movement significantly, making all-day sits worth the effort.

KNOW WHEN TO MAKE NOISE. Both rattling and calling are very effective in heavy undergrowth if hunting pressure is not a signifi-cant factor. Bucks feel comfortable responding to clattering horns or grunt calls in thick cover. Before and after the rut tone down rattling to imitate bucks just sparring, not actually fighting. But when you see evidence of scraping, put some "attitude" into your horn work.

TREE PRUNING. Shooting lanes are a necessity for the archer and a definite plus for the gun hunter, but keep them narrow and as incon-spicuous as possible. A mature whitetail will detect cut brambles within his home territory as quickly as you would notice car tracks across your front lawn.

THE RIGHT LOOK. Caliber is not particularly important when selecting a rifle for hunting the thick stuff. In fact, many hunters prefer a shotgun with slugs when working in such close quarters. Whichever you choose, keep that scope screwed down to its lowest magnification. Trying to get on a buck slipping through heavy cover at spitting range with a scope cranked to 10X defines futility.

DESIGNATED DRIVES. Drives can be effective in small patches of thick, dry cover, but attempting to drive in large chunks of heavy cover or wetlands is a waste of effort. A mature whitetail in heavy cover is already in the best sanctuary he knows. That makes him reluctant to bust loose. In large, heavy cover a mature whitetail will simply let drivers walk by, or if need be, circle behind them. ◈

From Outdoor Life, *November 1995*

Step by Step

by Mark E. Scott

*When the snow flies, it's time to climb down
from your stand and get on the right track.*

WE HAD JUST REACHED THE notch when my hunting buddy, Jeff Ladue, dropped his knee to the ground and motioned for me to take a look: There, in three inches of newly fallen snow, were the tracks of a large whitetail buck. We were in the first hour of our hunt, but we've killed brutes in even less time than that, so we moved slowly, one step at a time, scrutinizing the cover. The cold, still air amplified every noise.

Crunch, crunch, crunch. The buck exploded from his bed, just out of sight. We followed his tracks as fast as we dared, knowing that rutting bucks often lie down several times over the course of a day. In the next six hours, we jumped him two more times from his bed. But we never got a shot.

Through the morning and into the late afternoon, we followed that deer in a sweeping circle around the mountain. Just before dark, we found ourselves back in the notch where we'd begun our stalk. There, in the boot prints we'd made earlier, were the buck's tracks.

"He's just ahead," Ladue whispered. "I'll stay on the track. Why don't you circle back to where he came from this morning?"

I ran straight down the brushy hillside, heedless of the boughs slapping my throat, and swung left along the base until I hit a fresh track. I slowed, taking one, then two cautious steps, when a swish to the left caught my attention. Turning, I came eyeball-to-eyeball with one of the biggest bucks I've ever seen. I waited for him to step from behind a balsam fir tree and then dropped him with a single shot from my .270 pump. The 8-pointer tipped the scales at 240 pounds, dressed.

Preparing for the Hunt

"Yeah, but that was a lucky hunt," said one of my friends last winter when I told him the story. And yeah, he's right. But you make your own luck, and you do that by having the confidence to follow a track no matter where it leads. Larry Benoit, the legendary tracker from Duxbury, Vt., first taught me this many years ago as he pushed me deeper into the woods than I had ever gone before.

Most of this confidence stems from your skills as a woodsman, but a fair portion comes from concentration, and your concentration can be aided by the gear you carry. You want enough equipment to be (and feel) safe, but not so much that it hinders you on the trail. Wear light wool clothing and rubber pac boots; both are quiet and both will keep you warm in cold winds and wet conditions. Once you catch up to that buck, it may take you an hour to cover the next hundred yards. If it's late in the day, that long stalk could be worrisome. Bring extra food, waterproof matches, a flashlight and a space blanket in case you need to spend the night in the woods. Even with a light, it's virtually impossible to walk out of some softwood swamps at night. You're better off building a small shelter and waiting for daylight.

Carry two compasses. When you set out from the truck, dial one to an approximate return heading and tuck it away. For the second, pin a ball-compass on your jacket, and as you travel, glance at it periodically for your general heading. With the two, you can concentrate on finding that buck, instead of constantly wondering where you are.

Finding a Big Buck

As always, scouting is the key to taking a big buck. But instead of looking for deer sign, with tracking you want to scout the land itself. It all starts with maps. Trophy bucks seek out places that allow them to elude hunters, grow old and get big, which in the Northeast means large softwood swamps and remote mountaintops. Topo maps are good for locating big-buck areas, but I prefer the Delorme Gazetteers or state atlases because they help me find the big roadless areas quickly. What's more, these maps are updated frequently, showing me new roads and jeep trails that lead to areas where few hunters have ventured before.

After that, the best thing to do is to take a drive and familiarize yourself with the area. Learn firsthand how the mountains roll, where creeks and roads intersect. Find the best points of entry. You probably won't see a good buck, but don't worry, he's there. Right now, just gather the information you'll need when the snow starts falling.

Okay, so you've found your trophy area; now you need to know how to cut a track efficiently. Many hunters just zigzag up one side of the mountain, but the problem is, if the buck is bedded all day on the other side of the hill, you'll never cross him. A better way is to cover ground systematically, as the illustration (below) demonstrates. With a few well-planned movements, you should be able to cross the tracks of any buck moving horizontally or vertically on a mountain. If you don't, then it's time to hit the next spot.

Buck or Doe?

Let's say you cut a track. How do you tell for certain whether it's a buck or a doe? "If you trail a deer for 10 miles," as Larry Benoit told me years ago, "you darn well better know it's a buck." Just as bucks and does look different, their tracks appear different in the snow, particularly if the buck is pushing 160 pounds.

THERE'S A RIGHT WAY and a wrong way to cut a track. The hunter (a) who zigzags up the mountain wastes a lot of time blanketing a minimal amount of ground, while the other hunter (b) covers the whole mountain with less effort. Head for the notch first; it's an excellent travel route for rutting bucks and, on the way, you'll cut the trail of any deer crossing the mountain. Then work across the slope to find deer that have moved up or down. Repeat the process on the back side, and if you still haven't cut any tracks, hit the next mountain. Which one's the buck (right)? You be the judge.

127

A doe's track is generally smaller, and the front of her track sinks more deeply in the snow. With their slim necks and shoulders, does walk daintily, putting their feet down toes first and taking modest strides. In contrast, a rutting buck carries his weight in his shoulders and neck and his track splays outward because of his long, bull-legged gait. The bigger and older he gets, the more flat-footed he

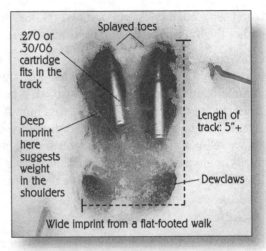

Splayed toes

.270 or .30/06 cartridge fits in the track

Deep imprint here suggests weight in the shoulders

Length of track: 5"+

Dewclaws

Wide imprint from a flat-footed walk

LEFT BY THE AUTHOR'S DEER, this track highlights six quick ways to identify a buck's imprint. Taken alone none of these clues guarantees that the track was made by a buck (for instance, a running doe will leave imprints from her dewclaws), but collectively, they're overwhelming evidence.

walks, leaving a wider imprint in the back of his hooves than a doe or young buck. To be absolutely certain the track is from a buck, follow it a little way. A trophy buck walks with a stagger, often dragging his feet. A doe, on the other hand, walks with one foot directly in front of the other. The illustration (previous page) shows the difference quite clearly.

Additional signs to look for are small, pea-sized urine stains in the snow. During fall, big bucks urinate frequently on their hocks, and the urine drips onto the snow. If you encounter a deer's bed in the snow, check where the deer positioned its hind legs. With bucks, you'll find yellow urine stains there.

The Final Stalk

The key to tracking a big buck is knowing when to go fast and when to slow down. The sign a buck leaves behind—a nose print in the snow, a long stride, a fresh scrape, a meandering walk—will tell you how to proceed. If a buck is on a destination march, most likely his stride will be long and his direction straight. He won't bother wasting much time rubbing a tree or freshening a scrape. Your only chance to see this buck is to put it in gear and hoof it as fast as you can, because even at a leisurely pace a mature buck can outwalk a hunter. The closer you keep yourself to a buck, the better the odds are that when he slows down, you'll be there to slide him a bullet.

On the other hand, if he's freshening scrapes or laying down new ones, he's on the prowl for a doe. When his tracks encounter tracks from other deer, it's time to slow down. He'll be nearby, on the move, chasing those deer.

Rutting bucks rarely stop for food, but when they do, it's usually to nibble on a mushroom or some lichen. After browsing, they invariably bed within a short distance. The instant you spot some feeding sign, put on the brakes. Get ready. Every step you take now is critical. Scan the woods in all directions. Before moving, look for places to step without breaking any twigs. Then, as you walk, keep your eyes searching in all directions. Most mature bucks will do a half-circle to check their backtrack before bedding down, and one second may be all the time you'll have to spot and shoot that big buck before he bolts.

Squeezing the Trigger

The Larry Benoits of the world are instinctive shots, giving little conscious thought to hitting big deer with open sights. The rest of us need to stay calm when we see a buck. Hurry, but stay relaxed and take a deep breath so you don't pull the shot. Someday everything will work just right. The tracks will lead you onto a mountaintop, and the snow will soften your approach. The buck will rise from his bed and stare at you, and you'll calmly squeeze the trigger.

Then you too will be looking for someone to help you drag your buck through the snow. ◆

From Outdoor Life, *December-January 1998*

Bucks at the Buzzer

by John Weiss

Deer season ends in three days and you haven't filled your tag. Don't panic—there are still tactics you can use before the clock runs out.

◆

O N THE SURFACE OF IT, A BANK robber and a deer hunter have little in common, yet I learned something from one particular holdup man that changed my hunting forever.

In the late 1950s, the infamous John Fitzsimmons held up a West Virginia bank. For two weeks he eluded more than 50 law enforcement officers in the rugged Monongahela National Forest. Yet shortly after the manhunt was abandoned, Fitzsimmons surrendered and returned the stolen cash. He also did not use a firearm in committing the crime—thus he received parole after 10 years in prison. Within hours of his release, though, Fitzsimmons robbed again and again fled into wooded land on foot. After a four-day search, authorities apprehended him, but one official admitted that probably the only reason they were successful was because this time they used dogs.

By way of explaining his Houdini-like disappearances, Fitzsimmons told a reporter, "When the heat's on, I know how to think like a deer." Once, according to Fitzsimmons, this meant belly-crawling into the leafy crown of a tree blown down by the wind. He lay there for three days, coming out only briefly after dark to drink from a nearby puddle of rainwater. Another time, he burrowed into a thick stand of honeysuckle and later told of a sheriff's deputy who passed by so close to his hiding location, "I could count the eyelets on his boots."

In the years since, I've thought about John Fitzsimmons many times. He usually comes to mind on the last day of deer season or on the last day of a hunt, when feelings of anxiety and desperation begin welling up within my gut because there is still no discernible sag in the camp meat pole.

No matter how many deer a hunter may decide to pass up, it quite often seems that as the season wanes, each and every one of those deer have evaporated into thin air. It's during these precarious, frustrating times that an almost eerie type of imagining takes place; I begin to picture John Fitzsimmons hunkered down in tall grass, thinking like a deer.

Thirty-nine states offer late deer seasons, where hunting may take place after December 15. The following strategies will help you put meat on the table, and leave the bank robbing to others.

Stay the Course

Many deer hunters faced with a slump elect to try something radically different. They are forced into a sort of desperate reappraisal because their best strategies have not produced. Occasionally last-minute changes are justified, but in most cases it's the wrong move.

On much private land and in remote backcountry areas, hunting pressure is not significant enough to force deer into hiding or cause them to severely alter their routines. In this type of situation, a hunter's lack of success can be attributed to nothing more than the fact that a buck has not yet ventured by his stand. If you know that hunting pressure has been minimal in your region, the wisest game plan is to stay the course. Muster enough confidence in your previous scouting efforts to tough it out on your chosen stand until the last minute of shooting light officially brings an end to yet another deer season.

Looking back over 30 years of pursuing whitetails, I can recall six different years in which I doggedly remained on stand and eventually took my buck during the final half-hour of the last day of the season. That amounts to six bucks, to date, that probably wouldn't have made it into my freezer if I had lost all confidence in my stand location and gambled on an entirely different region.

Whenever I'm attaching my deer tag to one of these latecomers, I'm always reminded of the useful mathematical principle known as reverse geometric progression. As applied to deer hunting, the principle works as follows: The longer you sit on a well-chosen stand without seeing anything, the better your chances become.

Deer Under Pressure

Obviously, public hunting areas, or areas that attract legions of hunters on opening day, require different end-of-the-season strategies. A good deal can be learned from the considerable body of research that attempts to explain how whitetails react to mounting hunting pressure.

One of the most revealing studies was conducted by Illinois biologist Don Autry. His report, "Movements of Whitetail Deer in Response to Hunting Pressure on Crab Orchard National Wildlife Refuge," describes the behavior of radio-collared deer that were monitored every day for seven months, including during the hunting season.

Autry discovered that whitetails seldom leave their home ranges, no matter how intense the hunting pressure. He noted only two instances in which they may leave, the most common being when they are chased by dogs. One deer in the study traveled 13 miles in an attempt to evade its canine pursuers. Yet shortly after the hounds were called off, the deer quickly returned to its home range. The other instance of evacuation came when the animal incurred an ultimately fatal wound during the hunting season; this behavior was attributed to shock.

It stands to reason that deer spooked by hunting pressure would choose to cling to the turf they are most familiar with, rather than venturing into unknown regions. However, research confirms that as hunting pressure intensifies within a given buck's home range, he can indeed be expected to travel to a so-called "safety zone" and begin adopting a low profile in terms of daily behavior activities. In Autry's research, the first two days of the hunting season resulted in deer sightings decreasing by 42 percent.

At this point, an enterprising hunter must search deeply into his reservoir of last-ditch tactics. Late in the season, he simply cannot allow his trousers to remain glued to his former stand in the hope that a buck will eventually come to him.

Where the Deer Go

Finding bucks that have retreated into seclusion means learning to think like a deer and being willing to penetrate those very places other hunters actually go to great lengths to avoid. In other words, imagine that you're a crafty buck (or someone who has just robbed a bank) and that your hide is in imminent danger of being hunted.

For three of the four days he was on the loose, outlaw John Fitzsimmons evaded his would-be captors and their dogs by wading long distances in shallow streams. Likewise, before wolves and big cats disappeared from the eastern portion of the United States, whitetails instinctively knew to take to the water to avoid predators hot on their scent. Hence, they ran into swamps, bogs, marshes and even swam rivers to reach the safety of islands. Today, the "predators" are either free-ranging dogs or hunters with guns—still, it's enough to keep the deer's water-loving instinct alive.

Not many deer hunters dress appropriately for cold-weather gunning in swamps. Fewer still have the desire to go sloshing through water and, occasionally, knee-deep black muck. As a result, most hunters find themselves bypassing such hellish places altogether or at least widely skirt their perimeters to stay on high and dry ground. Yet the serious hunter who is properly dressed will discover that shortly after opening-day rifles begin cracking, lowland areas containing at least several inches of standing water may begin acting as a magnet to deer. Hipboots are critical, as end-of-season temperatures in many states dip below the freezing mark.

Because of the combination of water and soft mire, moving quietly in standing water is as easy as tiptoeing through Jell-O. During the early and late hours of the day, you can expect to see deer on their feet. As the day wears on, however, they will seek out small hummocks and other slightly elevated areas of terrain where they can lie down on dry ground. A hunter who moves slowly, hunts into the wind and uses intervening standing timber to conceal each advance, often walks right up on bedded deer. If you miss your opportunity, don't despair. A retreating deer isn't likely to leave the swamp; indeed, he'll probably recede into its farthest reaches. Come back the next day, or even just a few hours later, this time entering the swampy real estate on the opposite side, and you can expect a repeat performance that may result in success.

Hunting midriver islands is even easier, but it requires the help of a partner and a lightweight boat. One of the hunters is dropped off at the upstream end of the island while his partner continues to float downstream and disembarks at the opposite end of the island. Then one hunter merely makes a drive toward the other.

A Premier Cropland Strategy

When the curtain is about to drop on your deer season, find a big cornfield adjacent to an expansive forest land where other hunters have been working—you will have pegged the whereabouts of at least several bucks.

Corn and deer go together like bacon and eggs. Standing cornfields offer deer everything they need in the way of readily available food and security cover. Yet staging drives through a cornfield is not tremendously effective, because a spooked buck is extremely reluctant to leave his chosen hideout. He'd much rather circle and dodge the drivers. So it's much better to hunt a cornfield buck one-on-one.

Keep in mind that late in the year, standing corn is dry and brittle. It's next to impossible to move through this sort of corn silently. Let's start with the knowledge that a buck is going to hear you. Therefore, the prime time to hunt a cornfield is when it's windy, making it an ideal tactic to use during midday as opposed to the usually calmer morning and evening hours. When the wind is loudly rustling the cured leaves and stalks of the corn, it covers any noises associated with your movements.

Don't make the mistake of hunting down one lengthy row of a cornfield—this leaves you readily visible from far away. Instead, hunt perpendicular to the rows by first poking your head between two cornstalks and then looking down the immediate row to your left and right. If you see nothing, step fully into the row. Then poke your head between two more cornstalks and again look down the next immediate row to both sides.

You needn't be concerned about prevailing wind direction; once air currents hit a cornfield, they scatter. A buck is likely to smell you, to be sure, but because he cannot determine which direction the scent is coming from, he'll lock up and hold tight. Suddenly, you'll find yourself peeping into the next row, and there he is—an easy 30-yard shot.

Once you've worked your way to the far side of the cornfield, hike down the length of the field for a distance of perhaps 75 yards and then begin working back in the opposite direction in identical fashion.

Hunt 'Em Like Rabbits

A mature whitetail is a woodland Houdini. Savvy hunters, therefore, live by two adages: A deer you can't see isn't necessarily a deer that isn't there; and secondly, if the cover is big enough to hide a rabbit, it's big enough to hide a deer.

Nowadays, many hunters are in fact pursuing deer in the same manner as they might hunt rabbits without dogs. This strategy is generally reserved for the final two days of the season—by then deer have shifted fully into survival modes and won't move unless spooked out of their cover.

In this scenario, hunters dress in bright orange clothing and spread out in a drive line to push through lengthy tracts of thick brush and vegetation. No standers are placed as in a conventional drive, though, because hard-hunted whitetails will not allow themselves to be pushed any significant distance. In fact, the drivers should space themselves no more than 15 yards apart or the deer won't run at all but simply hunker down and not budge an inch.

I recently participated in one of these "rabbit hunts" and was impressed with the results. Five of us spread out and began leisurely walking the length of a stream bottom where thick clumps of willows and tag alders offered perfect hiding conditions. We made no effort to quiet our footfalls and even carried on occasional conversation.

First a doe bounded out in front of us. She ran no more than 30 yards before quickly putting on the brakes and ducking back down again. Several minutes later a forkhorn buck popped up, which I brought down with a 20-yard shot. As we approached the downed deer, the same doe we'd previously flushed got up again, ran another 30 yards, and spooked a six-pointer farther ahead. That buck slinked along with his belly tight to the ground for a distance of only 50 yards before hitting the deck. One of my companions, Bob Wilson, visually marked his location, approached the deer with his shotgun already at his shoulder and took the deer with a neck shot from a scant 15 yards.

Larry Marchington, a deer biologist from the University of Georgia, tells of having similar experiences during the course of his research work.

"I've tracked radio-collared deer, knowing exactly where they were bedded. In walking toward them, they've often let me get so close I could see them breathing. There was one buck that allowed me to approach to within three feet of his hiding place, and he never moved a muscle. I slowly circled him, and he continued to just hug the ground. The only way I could get that deer to react to my presence was to make eye contact with him, and then he flew out of there."

Last Call

Finally, it's worth noting a potpourri of other locations where close investigations may reveal hiding deer. As you search, remember that the smaller the animal's dimensions the better—this means they probably haven't drawn the notice of many other hunters.

When logging crews harvest tracts of hardwoods, it's a common practice to bulldoze the remaining tree crowns, slash piles and cull logs into the nearest gully or ravine before replanting the area. This creates a latticework of thick security cover that shy and retiring bucks positively love.

Such gullies and ravines are invariably too tangled and often too dangerous to hunt through because of uncertain footing and the distinct possibility of branches breaking underfoot. Sneak-hunt along the upper rim overlooking the ravine, peering down into the cover for bedded deer. This is also a situation in which a whitetail hunter can take a page from the mule deer hunter's notebook. On occasion, toss a stone down into especially thick cover you can't see into. When the stone pings off logs and breaks dry branches, the commotion may rout out a nice buck.

Dr. Keith Causey, a professor of wildlife science at Alabama's Auburn University who has studied the responses of spooked deer during the latter part of the hunting season, has noted a curious trait. "In our radiotelemetry studies, we discovered that one type of spot where mature bucks like to hide is close to a rural residence where there is a good deal of human activity and even barking dogs in the yard, provided they are chained up and not running at large. Often, the deer bed in thick brush and tall grass, sometimes as close as 50 yards from the house."

Obviously this type of hunting requires the permission of the landowner and the utmost in safety precautions.

Lastly, use binoculars to glass large, wide-open meadows. Then take a closer look in hope of finding an isolated island of tall vegetation. This usually indicates a small patch of perpetually soupy ground the farmer prefers to skirt with his tractor and hay-mowing equipment to avoid getting stuck. The cover may very well be no larger in size than your kitchen floor, and it may be located 100 yards or more from the nearest woodlot edge. Nevertheless, if you've learned to think like a deer, wouldn't such an inconspicuous little hideout be the perfect place to hole up during the last hours of the hunting season? ◈

From Outdoor Life, *January 1992*

Deer on the Prowl

by Norm Nelson

If you've got a weak heart then read no further. But if it's unparalleled excitement that you want out of a deer hunt, then stillhunting is the only way to go.

T HE BIG WHITETAIL BUCK AND I badly startled each other. In the steady rain patter, he apparently didn't hear me until I'd stillhunted very close to his cedar clump shelter. I almost came unglued when he exploded into view, too spooked to even snort.

After the rifle's roar shattered the forest stillness, I heard a couple more rhythmic thumps as the by-now invisible deer continued bounding. So much for my semi-frantic snapshot.

But then came a distant, wood-splintering racket, followed by silence. Without snow, it took awhile to slowly, alertly follow up. I found the heart-shot buck. That terminal crash noise came from his failing to clear a windfall when the carburetor quit for keeps.

That's stillhunting at its best. Unlike the prolonged tedium of trail watching or waiting out a drive, stillhunting's uptight anticipation is an ongoing thrill. When the action does come, it's often sudden, without warning. Don't hunt this way if you have a weak heart.

Very old-timers like my 87-year-old father tell me that forest still-hunting was far more common decades ago. Maybe today's urban hunters don't trust their stealth and woodcraft skills. Although not an easy way to take woodland game, the bottom-line reality is that stillhunting can produce game when other tactics cannot.

Obviously, a lone-wolf hunter can't make drives to himself. Even when efficient manpower is available, effective drives require thorough knowledge of both the terrain and how local deer use it. If game chooses not to move because it fed well last night, lacks sexual ambition just now or doesn't like the prevailing weather, trail watching is usually hopeless.

The stillhunter is free of such vagaries. Instead of hoping game will come to him, he goes to it—although stillhunting is not the stalking of game already located. Tactically, he has two top priorities. First, to move quietly and alertly, his course basically dictated by wind, terrain and possibly sun direction. Second, to discover game before it sees, hears or smells him. The stillhunter must play a lone-hand game—two hunters seem to make not twice, but four times the noise of one hunter.

Slow movement is a must. A stillhunter covering ground too quickly simply can't look well enough for concealed game. He also can't help making extra noise to be picked up by critters who depend on acute hearing every day of their lives to stay out of trouble. They easily detect high frequency noises (including any rustles, squeaks or metallic clinks from our gear and garb) that we often can't hear.

The real trick in stillhunting is to do the looking and the moving as two separate functions. If you forget everything else, remember that! When you attempt to look for game and move your feet at the same time, sooner or later you will make unwanted noise—snapping a brittle twig, tripping noisily or whatever.

Don't follow any set rhythm of taking a set number of steps, then stopping. Instead, consider the area that you can see from where you stand as one vision zone. I never move until this zone, of up to 180° ahead and to both sides, has been totally studied.

A vision zone may range out only 50 feet in dense woods or 200-plus yards in more open country. Depending on the extent of the zone, terrain and cover, it may take 30 seconds or several minutes of methodical looking. Often a promising area is worth the time to just sit for extra eyeballing.

Don't expect to see a full-blown deer looming up ahead like calendar artwork. Look for just parts of the animal as clues. Most forest visuals are vertical lines—tree trunks, etc. An out-of-place horizontal line may be a log or the outline of a deer's back. Wide-field binoculars help greatly on such details.

Once, while hunting in the Cascade Mountains, my eye caught a tiny movement ahead. A broad leaf twitching with the breeze? But there was no breeze and, in that evergreen thicket, no deciduous leaves. I waited some minutes, then spotted the movement again for what it was—a doe's ear twitching as its owner listened. When she finally moved, right behind her came a shootable buck.

After searching a visual zone (and listening, too), select a route for the next few feet or yards, based on avoidance of brush contact or other potential noise. Footwork is important. Short steps are quietest. They offer best control of shifting your balance if you ease your foot down and feel a twig likely to snap under full weight. Also, only with short steps can you come down slowly and silently on your toes or the ball of your foot. Long steps force the heel down first, making it much more likely that you will snap twigs or make a soft but tell-tale thud.

Want some expert stillhunting lessons? Simply watch a house cat on the prowl for birds or field mice. Slow movement, long look-listen pauses, obvious patience and great concentration are what make felines the finest stillhunters in nature. Once, in Washington's mountains, I watched a mountain lion on the prowl. This best-of-all deer hunter resembles a magnified house cat at work.

Big or small, hunting cats are superb at using concealment. You should do likewise. Very often, unseen game ahead will hear you. By moving slowly with minimum noise, you may sound much like just another deer. But the listening quarry will be watching in your direction for visual confirmation. Don't slow yourself any more than necessary. I use camouflage makeup to make my pale face less visible against dark forest backdrop.

If you can move quietly in some kind of concealment, use that route rather than an easier-looking, more open course. Stick to shadows; avoid sunlit patches. When possible, hunt with the sun behind you. Go over ridgetops with caution, using brush or timber cover. If the hilltop lacks cover, try crawling. Of course, stillhunting must be done into the wind or at least across it—never downwind.

Often a stillhunter has the option of following fresh game tracks. Except under ideal conditions, such as new snow, one-man tracking demands so much attention that the stillhunter is distracted while he should be looking for actual game. More than once, deer have surprised me, costing me a shot simply because I was distracted by some interesting tracks. If you start trailing, remember that the maker of these tracks may be bedded down somewhere ahead and almost certainly watching his backtrail. To get anywhere close to it will require extremely good stillhunting.

The lay of the land can be friend or foe. Ridges and hills offer chances to surprise game on the other side. Flat country is tougher because it offers few elevation advantages to the hunter. Although knowing the area always helps, it's not truly essential for stillhunting. Once, a young stillhunter in our party, new to the place, nailed a whitetail buck the second morning. A fast learner, he capped that next year by pussyfooting close enough to a Cascades bull elk to take him with a bow.

The inexperienced stillhunter is often tempted to work mature ever-green timber, where dense shade means little underbrush. But closely spaced conifers self-prune their branches profusely, forming a noisy layer of dead twigs. Such forests can be hunted only when there's enough wind noise to cover the hunter's snap-crackle-pop progress. Unless soggy from rain or wet snow, dead leaves are another audio booby trap.

Some timber is open enough to have a good growth of clover or grass. By contrast, dense coniferous forests contain little ground-level browse to attract feeding game, but they then provide good escape cover when hunting pressure is on. In unseasonably warm weather, the cool shade of thick evergreen timber invites game. In cold weather, the evergreen canopy traps radiant ground heat for considerably warmer bedding than more open forests.

Where evergreen timber is lacking, game makes the best of thick brushy cover or tall grasses—the latter is commonly a deer favorite. In real cold or after rain, any warming sun draws game to south or west-facing slopes.

Best time of day for stillhunting depends on several factors. Stillhunting as early as light permits may find game feeding or on the move to bedding. Ground litter then is less noisy, thanks to the night's damp-ening dew. But if overnight frost has made fallen leaves ultra-brittle or has crusted the snow, better wait for some midday thawing.

Though rain or a moderate wind helps mask hunter movement sounds, strong winds are a mixed blessing. With their hearing impaired by too much wind, restless animals change location often rather than staying put. That aids the stillhunter, because moving game is far easier to see. But wind-jittery animals, up on their feet and watching for danger they can't hear, can spot the hunter more readily. Fortunately, a stiff wind covers his extra noise if the still-hunter sticks to thicker cover for extra concealment.

Worst of all are those dead-calm Indian summer days, when even your shadow seems to make a racket in the dried-out forest. The only option, then, is to hunt terrain where game can be spotted at a con-siderable distance (example: from one ridge to another).

Some cover simply can't be stillhunted. Swampy terrain is impossi-bly noisy, all the more if there's any ice to be broken. Dry, fluffy snow can be fairly quiet for walking. But typical autumn snow, heavy and wet, is composed of oversize, many-pointed flakes. Each step compression-shatters untold thousands of such crystalline flakes. That accounts for the appallingly loud squeakiness. Until it's settled, breaking its flakes in the process, such snow is no good for stillhunting. The settling process may take two or three days unless a thaw speeds it.

Snow characteristics may vary with terrain. North-facing snow is little affected by the weak sun of late autumn, but snow on southern and western slopes settles quickly with a few hours of sun.

The stillhunter must remember that weather affects game's likely location. The first serious snowfall often causes deer to hole up in the shelter of thick, low-branching evergreens, where they may stay 48 to 72 hours, believe it or not, even during the rut. Hungry when they finally leave cover, deer then are likely to feed during the day. But until they start moving, the pristine snow will be barren of tracks, leading to the false conclusion that all game has moved out.

Gear and clothing are critical in stillhunting. Soft leather boots with crepe soles are almost moccasin-quiet but treacherous in steep, wet or rocky terrain. Classic, Maine-style, rubber shoepacs make quiet steps. Their rounded sole edges are not as likely to shear-snap noisy twigs as stiffer, sharp-edged soles do. With any other rubber footwear, wear enough socks to prevent empty space around the foot from audibly pumping air at each step.

Harder, composition soles with lugs are necessary to maintain life and limb in rough country. Alas, such footwear is noisier. The only consolation is that in country steep enough to require lug-soled boots, the stillhunter has a longer "working range" across canyons, etc., and is not quite as vulnerable to making noise as the close-range, flatland hunter. At times, I've carried soft sneakers in my day-pack to slip on after climbing a ridge that demanded lug-soled, ankle-supportive boots. Another useful trick is to wear a pair of knit leg warmers running from knee-height to ankles. These muffle twig noise and grass swish.

Clothing choice is very simple. Whatever the material, it must be soft. Nylon, corduroy and stiff denim are too noisy. Wool and flannel are the great favorites for quiet movement. Some synthetics like orlon and acrylic are almost as good, depending on weave and nap. Rubberized raingear makes less noise than nylon or vinyl. Because a hat's brim snags noisy branches, wear a cap. Again, wool or knitted acrylic is quietest. I made a simple, woolen pack cover to keep my backpack from imitating a snare drum when I hunker through over-hanging branches.

For quiet carrying, a firearm's barrel length is more critical than weight per se. Although carbines are best, one of my favorite woods rifles has a 24-inch barrel. I find a 26-inch barrel is just too easy to bang against branches. A timber riflescope should have at least a 30-foot field at 100 yards—more would be better, because forest shots are often at close-range game on the run. Yellow shooting glasses contrast brown deer better against evergreen backgrounds.

Pocket hardware like keys, coins and cartridges must be handkerchief-wrapped to eliminate tell-tale clinking. When I rendezvoused with my deer-hunting daughter in the woods, her sardonic greeting was, "Hello, Santa!"

"Well before I saw you," she continued, "I could hear you playing 'Jingle Bells.' What's in your pockets?"

A ring of unwrapped keys, that's what. And deer probably could hear it twice as well as she could.

Although usually not physically taxing, stillhunting is tiring if you do it right. What wears you out is the strain of constant vigilance. And I mean constant! About the time you relax or daydream, up bounds a buck that makes good his escape because you weren't mentally prepared to react quite fast enough. But if you're a dedicated hunter, the high-tension hours of stillhunting are memorable whether you score or not. ◆

From Outdoor Life, *January 1990*

Snap Judgment

by *Gary Clancy*

If you want to be a trophy hunter, you'd better know how to quickly tell a really nice deer from one that'll make book.

◆

A NUMBER OF YEARS AGO, JUST about the time I was getting serious about hunting for big whitetails, Bill Jordan extended an invitation to me to join him on a hunt at the Perlitz Ranch in South Texas. Hunting South Texas had always been a dream of mine, so I jumped at the chance.

After two frustrating days in ground blinds with bow and arrow, I stashed the archery gear and pulled out the .25/06. On the third morning of the hunt, just as the sun was chasing the chill out of the mid-December dawn, a doe came dashing across the pasture in front of me, followed closely by a buck. Out of habit, I put my binoculars on the buck, even though I had already made up my mind that this was the deer I had come for. Before I could squeeze off a shot, another

Ear tips are 16-18 inches apart

Ear length of 6-8 inches

YOU CAN USE A BUCK'S EARS as a quick rack reference. A whitetail's ears measure about seven inches long and the tips are generally 16 to 18 inches apart. That would give this buck an inside spread of about 20 inches—a keeper in anybody's book.

buck eased out of the mesquite, sidled stiff-legged up to the first buck and, just like that, bone met bone and the battle was on. The adrenaline was already coursing through my veins, but now it did one of those volcano numbers, and all capacity to dispassionately appraise the trophy potential of either buck shot to the moon.

Eventually the issue was settled, with the vanquished buck skulking back into the brush. I took a deep breath, put the crosshairs on the victor and killed him. But when I got to where he lay, I felt sick to my stomach. What moments before had most assuredly been the trophy South Texas whitetail I had come for now lay before me as a spindly eight-pointer that I was ashamed to take back to the ranch. I vowed right then, kneeling in the sandy soil, my hands around a slender main beam, that I would do everything in my power never again to experience the emotions I was feeling at that moment.

In the years since, I've gotten pretty good at judging bucks quickly and accurately. Don't get me wrong. I can't glimpse a buck sneaking head-low through timber and tell you he'll score 163⅞ B&C. Nobody can. We're not talking "measuring," we're talking "judging" a deer in actual hunting encounters, which are often unexpected, fleeting and tension-filled. With practice, however, you can quickly and accurately determine whether or not the buck you're looking at is an animal that meets the standards you've set for yourself.

Ear Length

When viewed head-on or from the rear, a buck's ears make an excellent yardstick against which you can gauge tine and beam lengths. Whitetail ears average six to eight inches long; I split the difference and assume it's seven. A glance at the buck pictured on the facing page tells me that his main beams are roughly four times as long as his ear, or 28 inches. His brow tines are shorter than the length of his ears but his second tines are at least twice as long. I've seen enough—I'm shooting!

Ear Spread

When a buck faces you with his ears in the erect or cupped position, you can use the distance from the tip of one ear to the tip of the other as an indicator of his rack's inside spread.

Ear spreads measure between 16 and 18 inches, with the wider spreads generally found on large bucks in the northern United States and in Canada. Another quick look at the whitetail on the facing

ANTLER SPREAD is best judged head-on, is impossible to judge from the side and is always exaggerated when seen from the rear, especially when the ears are pinned back (left).

page tells me I'm seeing an inside antler spread of approximately 20 inches. Keep in mind that it's easy to overestimate antler spread when a buck is viewed head-on with his ears held back. A buck won't hold his ears in this position for very long, so if you're not sure whether he's a shooter, hold off for a moment, give him a chance to cup his ears and do the math.

Showstoppers

I'm fortunate to be able to spend 60 days or more each season hunting whitetails. But even with that kind of exposure, I still haven't seen enough big deer in the wild to become adept at judging them based solely on in-field experience.

The best way to learn how to quickly field-judge deer is to attend whitetail shows where mounted heads are on display. I often speak at seminars at these shows, and when I'm not on stage you'll find me strolling the aisles checking out the rows of mounted bucks with all the other whitetail nuts. But I'm easy to pick out of the crowd; I'm the one with the notepad and pen. I give a quick look at each head, study the antlers for five seconds or so and then write down what I think the buck will score. When I reach the end of the row, I go back and check my score against what's posted. When I began doing this, I missed the actual scores by an average of 13 inches. Now I'm down to five…if only my golf handicap would follow suit.

Body Language

No matter where you hunt, the best bucks in an area—those of true trophy caliber—will be at least 3½ years old. And because a buck can gain a deceiving amount in mass and antler configuration in just one year, it pays to be able to reliably distinguish mature from immature animals.

Yearlings, which are 1½-year-old bucks, are easily recognizable. Because they haven't attained the bulk that comes with maturity, their overall appearance bespeaks their age—slender build; delicate features; no sag in the belly or back; smooth, slick coat. Even during the rut, a youngest shows little swelling in the neck.

A mature buck is not easily mistaken either. In many cases, size alone is a valid guide. Mature bucks tend to be deep through the chest, lending the impression that they are short-legged. Expect to see some sag in the belly and a slight bow in the back. The head of a mature buck is blocky, and his eyes appear small and sunken. Older bucks also walk with a distinct, almost arthritic, stiff-legged gait quite unlike the fluid glide displayed by youngsters. During the rut, the neck of a mature buck is unmistakably swollen.

It's those in-between bucks, the 2½-year-olds, that are the confusing cases. They've begun to develop some of the bulked-up characteristics of mature deer, but they don't yet have the massive chests of their elders, nor will they display a significant amount of neck-swelling during the rut. Most 2½-year-olds already have that blocky look to their faces yet still retain the wide, liquid eyes of a yearling. More mistakes are made field-judging 2½-year-old bucks than are made with any other age group.

North Versus South

Body size can really throw off your field-judging. If you're a northern hunter accustomed to seeing mature bucks weigh in at 250

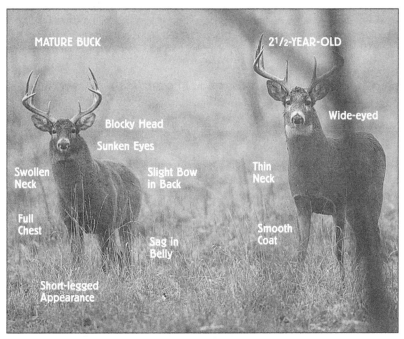

WHICH ONE'S THE SHOOTER? It's often difficult to distinguish between a mature buck and a 2½-year-old, but here body language speaks volumes. The mature buck is fuller through the chest, his coat is worn, there's a slight bow to his back and a sag in his belly, his head is blocky and his eyes appear sunken and smaller. He's your trophy.

JUST BEFORE DAWN ONE MORNING, a whitetail very similar to the one shown in picture (left) suddenly materialized out of a thin ground fog and walked broadside to me along a ridgeline. One glance at the buck moving through an opening in the trees was enough to convince me that he was a shoo-in for Pope and Young. Seconds later, when the buck stepped into another narrow opening, I launched an arrow. My aim was true, but when I later found the buck, I was shocked to see that he was a half-rack (right), one side snapped off three inches up from the base, probably in a fight with a larger buck or a collision with a vehicle—proving that snap field-judging is not a perfect art.

pounds or more, a good rack on a 130-pound South Texas whitetail is going to seem a lot larger than it actually is.

Southern hunters may have the opposite problem hunting in the North, where they're likely to underestimate deer. I can attest to that. Although I had hunted big-bodied deer in the northern United States and the Midwest all my life, the first time I hunted Saskatchewan I found myself underscoring bucks in the field by a good 10 to 15 inches. Only after I had killed a 160-class buck did I realize my error. That, however, is the kind of judging mistake I can live with.

From Outdoor Life, *September 1997*

MORE IN-FIELD SHORTCUTS

*E*XPERIENCED WHITETAIL HUNTERS CAN CATCH JUST A GLIMPSE OF A BUCK AND TELL YOU IF HE'S AN EIGHT OR 10-POINTER. HOW DO THEY DO IT? THEY'VE TRAINED THEMSELVES TO COUNT TINES ONLY ON ONE SIDE OF A RACK.

FORGET ABOUT THE MAIN BEAM AND BROW TINE, AND COUNT TINES. ASSUMING THE OTHER SIDE MATCHES, TWO TINES MEANS THE BUCK IS AN EIGHT-POINTER AND THREE TINES MEANS A 10 (like the buck pictured here).

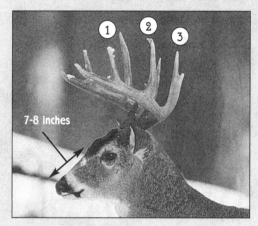

The Nose Rule

If you're looking at a buck from the side, forget about using the ears as a gauge. Instead, use the distance from the tip of his nose to his eye to estimate the length of the main beam and tines. On a mature buck, the distance from nose to eye is seven to eight inches. I go with the higher number, since most of the trophy bucks I've measured came in right at or very close to eight inches. On the buck above, that would give us second and third tines of about seven inches.

Eyeballin' Mass

Mass is the most obvious antler characteristic to judge. A buck with heavy antlers is easy to identify, as is the buck with spindly ones. But the bucks in the middle pose a problem. To separate the thick-beamed from the merely average, use the animal's eye circumference, which is about four inches, for comparison. If the main beams are as big, or bigger than, the eyes, that animal has decent mass.

Should You Take This Shot?

by George Haas

<u>*30 Questions for deer hunters.*</u>

───────◆───────

THERE HE IS. THE BUCK YOU'VE chased since opening day. He's big, he's broadside, and he's within range. So why wouldn't you shoot? And you shouldn't.

That and 29 other questions are posed by consulting editor George Haas in this quiz designed specifically for deer hunters. Not sure when to use doe scent? Or whether the .358 Norma Magnum is an appropriate deer cartridge? Take the test. But even if you don't come through with flying colors, be comforted in the fact that you've got a few weeks to bone up before you have to put your knowledge to the real test afield.

Q *You're hunting in open country and the buck on the previous page appears on top of a ridge. He's approximately 80 yards away, standing broadside, and yet you choose not to take the shot. Why?*

A Good call. If you miss—or if you hit solidly and the bullet goes through the deer—it will continue over the ridge and could hit a hiker, birdwatcher, farmer, or some other innocent. You do not have a safe backstop for your bullet.

Q *You're in a western state and have a choice of hunting deer in an old-growth (climax) forest or in an area that was clear-cut a few years ago and is now covered by low growth and patches of saplings. Which should you choose?*

A The aging clear-cut is the place to hunt. The very large trees of old-growth forest form a canopy that can almost completely cut off sunlight, effectively barring low growth. There's very little for deer to eat, hence very few deer. In a maturing clear-cut, however, there's lots of greenery for forage, and good cover, too.

Q *A stick bow is a) a Robin Hood–style longbow; b) a primitive bow made from a rough branch or sapling; c) a recurve bow; d) a and c; e) none of the above.*

A d) The term differentiates both longbows and recurves from compound bows.

Q *If all deer hunting (and deer killing of any kind) were stopped, the result would be a) an initial population explosion, then a crash; b) an initial population explosion, then a return to current numbers; c) a sustained population increase.*

A a) Human hunters have completely replaced natural deer predators in most of the United States. Nonintervention via controlled hunting would result at first in a vast increase in deer, but then numbers would plummet due to outright starvation and a generally weakened, disease-prone population.

Q *You are on a stand and make every effort to avoid moving. Suddenly, a red squirrel or a blue jay starts screaming and scolding only a short distance away. With all that racket, this is a great opportunity to stretch and scratch. True or false?*

A Very false. The squirrel, jay, or other woodland creature is used to you and isn't objecting to your unmoving presence. In fact, there's a very good chance that it's scolding an approaching deer.

Q *The simple, old-fashioned broadhead (one blade and two edges) is inherently less accurate than more modern arrowheads with two blades (four edges) or a three-bladed head (six edges). True or false?*

A True. The flat, one-bladed head is much more likely to "wind plane" and go off course.

Q *A small plastic bag that closes securely is useful on a deer hunt because it can keep the liver and heart clean and fresh while you haul your deer out of the woods. True or false?*

A False. Hearts and livers—especially livers—almost always spoil if they are placed warm in these airtight bags. Allowing them to cool before plastic-bagging is good, but using a net bag (like an onion sack) is better. Bloodstains won't kill you; a spoiled liver can.

Q *A key deer is a) another name for a dominant buck; b) a very small deer that inhabits some of the Florida Keys; c) a deer that is radio-collared and studied by biologists to determine the status of the local herd; d) none of the above.*

A b) These rare deer are very small, often weighing less than 50 pounds, and are now completely protected by law.

Q *A nice buck feeds alone every morning and evening in a sprawling alfalfa field, but you can't get within range. The buck seems to know he's safe out in the middle. Short of digging a pit blind and waiting for him, which the farmer won't permit, what can you do if you're hunting by yourself?*

A Stalk upwind. Move only when the buck's head is down with his eyes focused on the alfalfa. Freeze whenever the buck's head even starts to come up. Deer are sensitive to movement, not stationary objects.

Q *Hunting deer with any kind of handgun is a) a sad stunt attempted by an ego-tripping nitwit; b) a legitimate culmination of a hunt, if the hunter is skilled enough to stalk within truly effective range; c) the best and perhaps the only way to hunt if the terrain or very thick cover precludes the use of a shoulder firearm; d) all of the above.*

A d) But it is solely dependent on who is doing the hunting.

Q *Of the following cartridges, which are useful in North American deer hunting? a) .32 Smith & Wesson long; b) .25/20 Winchester; c) .38 special; d) .45 Colt pistol; e) .410 shotgun shell loaded with a slug; f) .358 Norma Magnum; g) none of the above.*

A g) The first five are inadequate and the .358 Norma is too much gun. There are many other nondeer cartridges. Investigate before you buy.

Q *The only real advantage arrows fletched in fluorescent colors provide is that they enable you to find them easily after a shot. True or false?*

A False. The fluorescent fletching enables you to better follow your arrow in flight, especially in dim light, often allowing you to see whether you hit your target or not.

Q *When hunting deer on horseback or muleback (which is legal in some southern states) with a buckshot-loaded shotgun, how can you improve your chances of finding deer?*

A By watching your horse's actions. Good deer-hunting horses and mules can often spot a deer (perhaps tipped off by smell) better than a man can. They stop and "point" the quarry with their heads or swivel their ears at the deer.

Q *You fire and the deer goes down, kicks a few times, and then lies still on its side with its legs pointing toward you. Confidently, you stride to the deer, put your rifle down, and make ready to gut it out. What's wrong with this picture?*

A Your life is in danger. A seemingly dead dear can disembowel a careless hunter with its sharp hooves. Approach from the rear with a loaded rifle ready. The usual test is to touch the eye with the rifle's muzzle. If the deer does not react, it's almost certainly dead.

Q *Shooting a deer or any other large mammal with a "full patch" or "full metal" jacketed military round is a very poor idea as well as illegal almost everywhere. Why is it counterproductive?*

A Full-jacket military rounds, usually sold as military surplus, tend to put the bullet right through game, leaving a very small wound channel that doesn't immediately kill or disable unless a vital organ is hit.

Q *The .357 Magnum revolver is seldom used nowadays for deer hunting. Why?*

A Because its energy level is so low. Authorities say it should only be used by very good shots, and most very good shots use something more powerful such as the .44 Remington Magnum or an even more powerful round.

Q *Bolt-action rifles are on average more accurate than semiautos, pumps, and lever actions. However, in one type of terrain they are not the best choice. What is that?*

A In close-range, brush-country hunting, shots must often be taken very quickly, and sometimes a quick second shot must be fired at a wounded animal. For this, semiautos, pumps, and lever actions—particularly those with short barrels—are faster, and they are plenty accurate at moderate ranges.

Q *When you're tracking a wounded deer on hard, dry ground, how can a roll of toilet paper or packet of facial tissue prove to be extremely useful?*

A On this type of terrain, you're relying for the most part on blood spots—rather than tracks—to provide evidence of your quarry's route. Since these spots may be few and far between, marking the blood with pieces of paper will help you find the established trail quickly each time you lose it looking for sparse sign ahead.

Q *The deer has been gutted out and now you want to hang it to cool. Should you hang it head down or head up?*

A Hang it head down, so that remaining body fluids flow forward into the neck and head, not into the hams. These fluids, particularly blood, can taint the flavor.

Q *In thick cover you must frequently shoot deer at quite close range. What is the best type of sight for thick cover?*

A A low-power scope in the 2x or 2.5x range, which enables faster target pickup than traditional V-notch sights. A peep or aperture sight, incidentally, ranks just behind the low-power scope.

Q *You have been a bit wild with your knife and left deer hair all over the skinned-out carcass. And hair burned on the meat while cooking sure does taint the flavor. What's the easiest way to remove it?*

A Use a wide roll of Scotch tape to dab at the hairs. The hairs stick to the tape and are easily pulled off. Do this before the surface dries and have tweezers ready for stubborn hairs.

Q *Hunting whitetails using hounds to drive them to standers is a technique once popular in the United States, but it has long since been outlawed. True or false?*

A False. The practice is still legal and popular in some southern states where deer are extremely abundant and where very heavy swamp cover makes conventional methods less viable for thinning the herd.

Q *You regularly shoot a scoped .30/30 Winchester lever-action rifle in your home state and do well with it, but you're going to open country out West for mule deer. Will your rifle be adequate?*

A Not if you expect to make long shots. If you sight in the 150-grain .30/30 load to be dead on at 150 yards—a reasonable choice—you will be approximately one foot low at 250 yards and an incredible two feet low at 300. You need something in a gun that shoots flatter.

From Outdoor Life, *September 1995*

Classic Whitetail Stories

Salmon River Whitetail

by Jack O'Connor

One shot ended my lifelong search for a major big-game trophy I did not have.

———◆———

THE NORTHERN VARIETY OF THE whitetail deer in its various forms is the most widely distributed big-game animal in the United States. Found from Maine to Oregon, it furnishes more sport to hunters than any other big-game animal and is responsible for the sale of more rifles and ammunition for the manufacturers and more telescope sights for the scope makers. And, because sportsmen buy licenses to hunt it, the money it brings in keeps most game departments functioning.

But until recently the Northern whitetail was to me as strange a trophy as the greater kudu, the desert bighorn, and the ibex are to most hunters. I have hunted all of these fine animals and others just as exotic, but the Northern whitetail had always eluded me.

Of all the varieties of Northern whitetails the one least known is the one found in the Northwest. The more plentiful mule deer and the elk sell the out-of-state licenses and get the publicity. In fact, many hunters do not even realize that some of the largest whitetail deer in North America and some of the best trophies come from the Northwestern states of Idaho, Washington, Montana, and Oregon, and from the Canadian province of British Columbia. These Northwestern whitetails are probably just about as heavy as the famous whitetails of Maine, and their heads compare favorably with those of whitetails shot anywhere. The No. 4 listing in the 1964 edition of Records of North American Big Game is a whitetail shot in Flathead County, Montana, in 1963, and I have seen handsome and very large antlers nailed to barns and garages and poorly mounted on walls of backwoods bars and country stores. Mostly these big whitetails are taken not by trophy hunters but by backwoodsmen and farmers who are after meat. These whitetails of the Northwest are classified *Odocoileus virginianus ochrourus*.

I grew up in the country of the Northern whitetail's little Southwestern cousin in the Sonora, Arizona, or Coues whitetail. I have hunted these fine deer in Arizona, in Sonora, and in the Big Bend of Texas, and I have taken many handsome bucks of this diminutive species. Such small skill as I have at hitting running game I owe to the Arizona jackrabbit and the Arizona whitetail. I have also shot the small but quite different Texas whitetail found around San Antonio. But a good Northern whitetail was one of the few major North American trophies I did not have.

I had never laid eyes on a Northern whitetail until I moved from Arizona to Idaho more than 20 years ago, and then it took me about three years to see one. I'll never forget the first one I saw. I was hunting pheasants with a wonderful Brittany spaniel named Mike. He had been cruising through a field of rich golden wheat stubble when he went on point at the edge of a grassy swale. I thought he had pinned a cock pheasant, but when I got up to him he looked at me out of the corner of his eyes and wore the sneaky expression he assumed when he was doing something he knew he should not do.

I picked up a stone to flush whatever it was, and threw it at the spot in the grass where Mike's nose was pointed. Out burst a little white-tail doe. Most dogs are convinced that they have been born to be deer and rabbit hounds, but Mike almost fell backward in surprise. Another time Mike hauled up on the edge of a brushy draw on solid point. I walked in, kicked the brush. A pair of cackling roosters came barreling out. I shot, dropped one of them, was about to take the other when a big whitetail buck sailed out of the brush and headed across the stubble toward a patch of woods. For the rest of the bird season, which mostly at the time ran concurrently with the deer season, I carried a couple of rifled slugs in my pants pocket so that if I jumped another whitetail I could jerk out a shot shell and slam a shell loaded with a slug into the chamber. But the news must have got around; I never saw a buck.

A farmer I knew told me he just about had a big whitetail buck tied up for me. He said that the old boy lived in a canyon that bounded one of his wheatfields. That buck fed on wheat all summer and in the fall feasted on the sweet, stunted little apples that fell in an abandoned orchard in one corner of his place.

So I spent about 10 days hunting him off and on during the season. His tracks were everywhere—in the orchard, in the wheat stubble, along the deer and cattle trails among the brush and trees, and on the bank of the little trout stream that ran through the bottom of the canyon.

Keeping the wind in my favor, I stillhunted cautiously and quietly along the trails, taking a few steps, stopping, listening, watching. Once I heard something moving quietly off through thick brush, and I found his bed below a ledge in a warm spot where the sun had melted the frost off the grass. Another time I heard a crash below me and caught a glimpse of his white flag flying. I sat for hours with my back to a tree waiting for him to show up. He didn't.

"I can't understand why you can't see that buck," my farmer friend said. "I seen him yesterday when I was looking for a stray cow, and Bill Jones seen him from his pickup when he was coming back from getting the mail four or five days ago. Said he wasn't a danged bit wild; stood there looking at him. He could have hit him with a slingshot."

*A*nother year, while scouting for good pheasant areas in eastern Washington, I found a pretty little valley full of trees and brush and with a clear brook wandering through it. It lay between two grassy hillsides that ran down from rolling wheatfields. The valley was full of pheasants. The hillsides supported several coveys of Huns. Quail roosted in the trees. And the valley also contained a herd of whitetails. I saw a doe, a fawn, one small buck, and also the tracks of a big buck.

I made up my mind to be in a strategic spot in the valley as soon as it was light enough to shoot on opening day. So when the day came I parked my station wagon along the road half a mile from the valley and left my Model 21 Winchester 12 gauge and my puzzled, whining Brittany spaniel locked up. Wearing a pair of binoculars around my neck and carrying a light 7 x 57, I walked through a wheatfield toward the head of the valley. I was almost at the spot I had in mind when I heard the crash of rifle fire. A startled doe streaked by me. Running along the grassy hillside and up into the wheat stubble were the dim forms of about a dozen deer flaunting white tails. I sat down and got them in the field of the binoculars. All were does and fawns. Then something caught my attention just under the skyline about a quarter of a mile away. I put the glasses on whatever it was. It was a big buck sneaking along. When he topped out I saw heavy antlers.

About 20 shots had been fired, but now the last deer was out of sight. I could hear voices coming from the valley. It was quite light now. I walked a little farther. Then I saw four men gathered around a small and very dead buck. One was gutting him. I talked to the men a few minutes. Before long they departed in triumph, each holding a leg of the buck. I went back to my car and stowed the rifle and the binoculars. Then I let my joyful dog out and set off to see if I could have any luck on birds.

In Arizona and Sonora the Coues deer are found high. In southern Arizona they are seldom lower than the altitude where the evergreen oaks the Mexicans call encinos grow—about 4,000 to 4,500 feet. The desert variety of mule deer are out in the mesquite and cactus of the flats and the low rolling hills. Out on the flat Sonoran desert west of the railroad that runs south from Nogales, Arizona, the mule deer are on the perfectly flat sandy arboreal desert where they range among the mesquites, ironwoods, and chollas. Low hills and little ranges rise from the desert floor, and on all of them are (or used to be) whitetails. Sometimes the whitetails are in easily navigable foothills of the tall, rocky, desert-sheep mountains.

But in the Northwest, at least in areas with which I am familiar, whitetails are found lower than the mule deer, on the brushy hill-sides near wheatfields, and in the wooded riverbottoms back in the elk mountains. They are bold but furtive, and they'll live all summer in a farmer's woodlot.

Some of them grow to be very large. I once knew a man who ran a meat locker in Lewiston, Idaho, my home town. He told me that the heaviest buck ever weighed at his plant was a whitetail. As I now remember he said its field-dressed weight was around 335 pounds. I have heard of Northwest whitetails in Washington as well as Idaho that were about as heavy. I have never seen a deer of any sort that I thought would dress out at anything like 300 pounds, but now and then one undoubtedly turns out to be that heavy.

I started closing in on my first Northwestern whitetail in the fall of 1969 when my wife and I drove to the ranch of our friend Dave Christensen on the Salmon River downstream from Riggins, Idaho. Dave operates an elk-hunting camp on Moose Creek in the Selway Wilderness Area and lives most of the year on the beautiful Salmon River ranch. When I first knew the elk-hunting camp it was Moose Creek Lodge, a luxurious bit of civilization out in the wilderness. A hunter could go out after elk all day and return at night to a drink around a fireplace, a good meal served with silver and linen, a hot shower, and a sound sleep on an inner-spring mattress. But the area was declared a wilderness. The federal government bought the lodge and burned it down. Now in the fall Dave's dudes fly in to a U.S. Forest Service landing strip a few miles away and hunt elk from a comfortable tent camp near the spot where the lodge used to be. I have shot five, six, and seven-point elk out of Moose Creek. Dave and his father Ken took the money they got from the sale of the lodge and their land and put it into the Salmon River ranch.

*A*s my wife and I drove in that November day in '69 we saw a whitetail buck in a field a mile or so from the ranchhouse. Not long afterward we saw some whitetail does and fawns.

"You must have a lot of whitetails around here," I said when Dave came out to meet us.

"Plenty," he told me. "The whitetails are mostly low down along the creek and in the brushy draws that run into it. The mule deer are higher."

The season around Dave's place was closed then, so my wife and I had to forgo the whitetails. We hunted mule deer in another management area about 20 miles away. But we made a promise to take a run at the whitetails.

Along in August, 1971, Dave called me.

"You haven't forgotten our date to hunt whitetails?" he asked. "No? Well, the season opens October second. Drive down the afternoon of the first and we'll have at them."

My son Bradford, who is outdoor editor of the *Seattle Times* and who is a long-time pal of Dave Christensen and his wife Ann, flew from Seattle and joined us on the drive to the ranch.

One of Dave's successful elk hunters from Moose Creek had come down to the Salmon to try for a deer, and three other hunters who were on their way into Moose Creek for elk were camped down the creek a mile or so from the ranchhouse.

The strategy was simple. Eleanor, Bradford, and I, accompanied by a guide named Stan Rock, would climb about 1,000 feet above the ranch near the head of a canyon that carried a little stream that ran into Dave's creek. After giving us time to get into position, Dave would walk up the canyon on a deer-and-cattle trail that ran along the bottom. There were whitetails and mule deer in those canyons, and with luck we should get some shooting.

It was dark and chilly when we started out, and the sun was not up when we arrived near the head of the canyon. We were high on a grassy ridge. The canyon dropped sharply below us, and the bottom was a tangle of trees and brush. The far side of the canyon was steep, mostly rocks with a few low bushes and sparse grass.

Eleanor had gone on to the brink of the canyon. Bradford was 20 feet or so to her left. I was in the process of filling up the magazine of an old pet .270 I had used from northern British Columbia to Botswana and Iran. It is a pre-1964 Winchester Model 70 Featherweight stocked in plain but hard French walnut by Al Biesen of Spokane and fitted with a Leupold 4X scope on the now-obsolete Tilden mount. It has the original Winchester barrel with the original Featherweight contour. The only thing Biesen did to the metal was to put the release lever for the hinged floorplate in the forward portion of the trigger guard and checker the bolt knob.

This is a terrific rifle. I bought it from the Erb Hardware Company of Lewiston, Idaho. Year after year it holds its point of impact. Carry it in a saddle scabbard, jounce it around in a hunting car on safari, ship it a few thousand miles by air, let it get rained on for hours in a Scottish deer forest, shoot it at sea-level or at 10,000 feet, in the crackling heat of the Kalahari desert or under the glaciers in the sub-arctic Stone sheep country of British Columbia and it always lays them in the same place. It is also one of those rare light sporters that will group into a minute of angle if I am using good bullets and do my part.

J had just finished slipping the last cartridge into the chamber and putting on the safety when Eleanor, who has eyes like an eagle, said, "Deer...two deer. The lower one's a buck."

Two deer were scooting up the far side of the canyon about 225 to 250 yards away. Both were waving big white tails. I could dimly make out antlers on the lower one.

The sight of those flaunting flags across the canyon made me shed 25 years. Once again I was back in my favorite Calelo Hills along the Mexican border of southern Arizona, where I had some small reputation among the local yeomanry of being a fair hand on running whitetails. I sat down quickly, put the intersection of the crosswires just to the left of the buck's head for lead, and squeezed the trigger. So far as results went, it was almost as spectacular as a brain shot on an elephant. The buck fell, started rolling, and tumbled clear out of sight into the brush and timber at the bottom of the canyon.

"Some shot!" said Bradford.

The buck was a big one. It had long brow points and four points on each beam—a four-pointer Western count, a 10-pointer Eastern count. He had been hit rather far back through the lungs. Down there in that narrow canyon it was so dark that the exposure meter said half a second at F.2 would be about right. Since we had no flash, good pictures under those conditions were impossible. Later someone would come out from the ranch with a packhorse and get him.

By now the sun was up and bright, and while the others went along around the head of the canyon where I had shot the buck and to the head of the next, I stayed behind admiring the scenery. Far below, the little creek glistened through the timber along its banks and as it twisted through the meadows. The meadows were still green, the pines dark and somber, but along the creek cottonwoods and willows were shimmering gold, and patches of crimson sumac blazed on the hillsides.

Up in the high country at the head of the creek, ridges where the Salmon River elk ran, an early storm had frosted the dark timber with snow. Far below against the green of a pasture I saw some moving black dots. The glasses showed me I was looking at a feeding flock of wild turkeys.

Clear down in the bottom of the main canyon I heard a fusillade of shots. I made a mental note that they were probably fired by the Californians who were going to try for deer before they went in to Moose Creek for elk. I hurried to catch up with the other O'Connors, who were out of sight over a ridge.

I heard two quick shots. Then I saw Eleanor and Bradford, rifles in hand, sitting on the hillside looking down.

"Get anything?" I asked.

"Buck mule deer, sort of a collaboration," Bradford said.

"The heck it was," Eleanor said. "I shot behind it and then Bradford dumped it. See? It's lying down there on the road."

The glasses showed me a young buck mule deer close to 300 yards away.

When we returned to the ranchhouse we found that the Californian had taken three whitetail bucks out of a herd of eight. The largest had heavy antlers with three points and a brow tine on each side. Though their measurements were the same as those of my deer, this buck appeared to be heavier. The next buck was somewhat smaller than mine and the third was a youngster.

Soon a packhorse came in with my buck. He and the largest buck shot by the Californians measured 18 inches in a straight line from the top of the shoulder to the bottom of the brisket. Both were fat and in fine condition. We had no means of weighing them, but I have weighed many mule deer with the same measurements and they have weighed between 185 and 195 pounds. These two whitetail bucks in weight and measurements were every bit as large as typical large four-point mule-deer bucks.

I was interested in comparing them to Arizona whitetails I had hunted so long. They were just about twice as large, since an average large, mature Arizona whitetail will weigh from 90 to 110 pounds. As is true among Arizona whitetails, the top of the tails of the old bucks is a grizzled brown whereas the upper portion of the tails of the young bucks is bright orange. Oddly, the tails of these big bucks

MEMORIES OF LONG EXPERIENCE flash through mind as the camera records end of elusive mission—my 10-point Northern buck.

looked to be the same size as those of their Southern cousins.

The beams of my buck's antlers were a bit over 23 inches long, and the inside spread was 18 inches. I have never shot an Arizona white-tail with beams anything like that long, but I did take one once that had a 20-inch spread. Though the Northwestern whitetail is twice as heavy as his Southwestern cousin, his antlers aren't twice as large. The coats of the big deer were a bit more brownish and less grayish than those of Coues as I remember them. The young Northwest whitetails have much more grizzled coats than those worn by young Arizona whitetails. These are quite bluish.

Sad to say, my underprivileged wife didn't get another shot. We drove up a precarious ranch road late that afternoon and early next morning when the deer should have been moving. We hunted the heads of several canyons and glassed the points and ridges, but all we saw were does and fawns. The bucks had got the message. ◆

From Outdoor Life, *February 1972*

My Whitetail Quest

by Jim Zumbo

"My sights were set pretty high. I figured a whitetail that scored above 155 would satisfy my quest."

◆

WHEN I THINK OF PLACES TO hunt big whitetails, a couple of regions come to mind. Perhaps foremost is Western Canada, but south Texas ranks right up there as well, along with places in the Lake States and the Midwest.

A couple of years ago I'd decidcd to dedicate a season to taking a trophy whitetail—a buck far better than anything I'd tied my tag to in almost 40 years of hunting these wary deer. At the time I made that vow, my best whitetail was a pretty 10-pointer I shot in Tennessee that scored 140 Boone and Crockett Club points.

I set my sights pretty high. I figured a buck that scored above 155 would satisfy my quest. But accomplishing that feat would take some doing. Lots of doing.

So where did I start this journey? With all due respect to the Lone Star State, I opted for Alberta and Saskatchewan. Whitetail buffs need no briefing on these two provinces; each annually produces giant whitetails and the odds of taking a record-book buck are much better there than in the U.S.

My first hunt was in Alberta, because outfitter Harvey McNally of Cadogan had been pestering me for a couple of years to hunt with him. I took him up on his invitation and soon learned that McNally is a little crazy, but not in the literal sense of the word. He's crazy because nothing stops him when he's looking for a big whitetail. Not snow, ice, arctic winds, or treacherous roads will divert him.

A Hard Place

McNally loves to sit at a place fondly known as "The Rock," which is, you guessed it, a big rock. The rock sits high on a hill overlooking a vista of pasture and thick aspen bush, which is what most of that part of Alberta is composed of.

It matters that the rock is high on the hill, because when the wind blows, any sitter on the rock becomes a helpless victim. Remember, this is November in Canada. Nevertheless, you sit obediently on the rock because many of McNally's hunters have collected huge whitetails there. I shut up and stayed put without whining.

I was approaching advanced hypothermia when a magnificent 10-point buck sprinted across a pasture and headed straight for the slope on which the rock sat. There was one minor problem: in front of us the slope was covered with one of the thickest aspen stands in Alberta. The buck, of course, never reappeared, and that was that.

Bushwacked

Another day, McNally and I stood in a cleared seismic strip and watched an equally impressive buck race madly after a doe. They were traveling roughly toward a cleared strip, so we ran to intercept them.

We had gone almost 800 yards when I spotted a deer standing just inside the bush looking at me. I couldn't identify it in the thicket, but when it suddenly whirled and ran, I saw enough. A huge rack graced his head, and that was that.

Toward the end of the hunt a third mega-buck showed up, this time on a drive with Kevin West, one of McNally's guides. West and his dad own a big farm loaded with trophy whitetails, and our entire party worked the drive, including Harvey and the other guides, and all the hunters.

I had just taken my assigned position when I saw a half-dozen deer trotting out of the drive area. The last deer, a tremendous buck, took my breath away. He was, and still is, the biggest whitetail I had ever seen in a lifetime of hunting. Unfortunately, he was 600 yards away. All I could do was hyperventilate. Our party looked for him the rest of the day, but no dice.

Summing up the hunt with McNally, I passed up a half-dozen eight- to 10-point bucks, but nothing that was really interesting. I kept the faith that the big one might show up in range at any time. It didn't.

My quest continued. I turned my pickup east and headed to Saskatchewan. My good pal, Greg Severinson, who is manager of Cabela's Outdoor Adventures, had arranged a hunt with Saskatchewan outfitter Brian Hoffart. Severinson would be in camp to hunt during a couple of days of my stay.

For the most part, Saskatchewan only allows resident Canadians to hunt the southern half of the province. This is agriculture land, and a haven for big bucks—Milo Hanson took the world-record typical whitetail there in 1993. The northern region is heavy bush country, so it's tougher to hunt, but it too is loaded with huge whitetails.

Severinson, who is a skilled whitetail hunter, was all smiles when he returned to camp after the first day of hunting. Hoffart had rattled in a whopper 171 B&C buck on their first attempt and Severinson killed it. It didn't help my frame of mind that Severinson had seen another whopper buck on the way out of the woods, because he loved to rub it in.

I had plenty of luck on that hunt, all bad. Giant tracks in the snow betrayed the presence of several fine bucks, but the deer remained unseen in the heavy bush. The most memorable event was my all-day stint in a tree stand during zero-degree temperatures. I sat there from first to last light and never came down. I'd never done that before in my life, and I'll never do it again. I sat there, patient and freezing, and all I saw was one buck, a little forkhorn. And so,

AFTER TWO YEARS OF TRYING, Zumbo finally took the buck of his dreams, this Saskatchewan 10-pointer that scored 159 Boone and Crockett points.

when the first year of my whitetail quest ended, I hadn't fired a shot.

I went back to McNally's the next year and once again drew a blank, though I had again seen a couple of huge bucks. As always, they were too far away or simply vanished in the bush. However, McNally offered two deer, one whitetail buck and a muley buck, and I connected with a dandy four-point muley.

One of the whitetails we had spotted was chasing a doe over a ridge, so McNally and I gave chase immediately, which meant running full steam around the bottom of the ridge, hoping to intercept them on the other side.

When McNally runs, there's no stopping him. As I said, he's a little crazy. By the time we got around the hill, the deer were gone, which was just as well, because I was out of breath big time and my eye-glasses were hopelessly fogged.

McNally occasionally hunts out of an elevated wooden stand that overlooks some big buck runways. When I'm scheduled to hunt with him, he sees big bucks before and after I hunt, but when I'm in the blind, we might as well be on the moon. Absolutely nothing happens. As during the year before, I'd passed a few bucks that I'd have shot anywhere—except Canada.

Again I headed east in my pickup, pointing it toward Saskatchewan, and this time I had a feeling that my Canadian whitetail jinx would end. Severinson was again in our party which this time was run by outfitter Pat Baucus. And Severinson didn't even wait for the first day to shoot a big buck, as he'd done the year before. He showed up with a beauty on his truck, a 164 B&C buck that he'd taken with another Saskatchewan outfitter. (Saskatchewan allows two whitetail bucks in most northern areas.)

He was all set to rub another dose of salt into my old wounds, but before he could, I got back at my old buddy and fulfilled my quest. It happened on the first morning when I was sitting on stand. A huge buck suddenly materialized out of the bush, and it didn't take any pondering to judge his worth. I reacted instantly, and went home with the biggest buck of my life. The deer scored 159.

You can bet I'm going back to western Canada for big whitetails. Although I finally got the buck I wanted, other places are waiting to be discovered, like Manitoba and parts of British Columbia. Knowing the tremendous bucks that are out there, it won't be long until I renew my quest. ◆

From Outdoor Life, *June 1995*

Muzzleloader Deer Hunt

by Charles Elliott

Our respect for the pioneers soared as we struggled to keep our powder dry and tried to outsmart a big buck.

———— ◆ ————

WHY SHOULD THIS PARTICULAR buck," I asked, "be endowed with more intelligence than its brother stags in this vicinity?"

"It's not brains," Howard Verner said, "but pure, cussed luck."

Jack Crockford, third member of our party, looked up from his flint-lock rifle, the barrel of which he was wiping down with oil.

"I guess the buck wouldn't call its luck cussed," he said, "if it keeps his hide unpunctured."

Up to this point, all the breaks had gone in favor of the whitetail on which we had concentrated for the better part of a week. One factor in the deer's favor was that our modern, high-powered rifles were locked in dry gun cabinets at home and that we were armed with primitive muzzleloaders. Another was the weather, which for four solid days had not been fit for any creature without gills.

In this one week, my respect soared for the buckskin-clad frontiersmen, who retained their scalps and kept their paunches full of red meat.

All of this had started the Sunday before, when we pulled into the Game and Fish Commission's checking station on Warwoman Road above Clayton, in northeast Georgia, and bought our $5 permits for one of the most unusual hunts in which it has been my privilege to participate. This was the area's second annual primitive weapons hunt, held October 24-29, 1966. "Primitive weapons" meant that you could take a whitetail of either sex with any rifle or shotgun loaded from the muzzle end, or with bow and arrow.

By the time we arrived, some 30 Daniel Boones and Davy Crocketts had already registered for the hunt, but no Robin Hoods had yet appeared.

As we talked with George Speed, manager of the Warwoman Management Area, I showed him my gun, a .50-caliber flintlock with a 36-inch octagonal barrel. It was a custom job, built for me by Jack Crockford. I asked how many of the hunt applicants had brought original rifles.

"A few have checked in with guns a century and a half old, or older," George said. "But yours looks as if it might knock over a whitetail with the best of them."

My companions were the man who made my rifle, Jack Crockford, 43-year-old assistant director of the Georgia Game and Fish Commission; and Howard Verner, who runs an electrical supply and maintenance business at Norcross, above Atlanta, and is a couple of birthdays short of the half-century mark.

Jack is a top deer expert. He has had more to do with bringing the deer herds back to Georgia over the past score of years than any other man I know. He is the fellow who conceived and helped to develop the Cap-Chur Gun, a CO_2 weapon that shoots hypodermic needles instead of bullets. He first used it in deer-management work, and more recently it has become a game-management tool all over the world. One of its chief claims is the salvation of the white rhino herd in South Africa.

It's only natural that buck hunting is Jack's first love. He can read tracks, skinned trees, and other sign and almost tell you how an old stag is thinking. For his age, Jack has taken more whitetails than any other man of my acquaintance.

Jack's wife says that he was born 150 years too late. For the past decade, he has gone in for muzzleloading rifles, building them with the same care and precision that the old Pennsylvania gunsmiths must have used a century and a half ago. The flintlock Jack put together for me is a thing of beauty. Old Dan'l Boone and his contemporaries would have been proud to carry such a gun in the Kain-tuck' wilderness.

It is a replica, of course, and about the only change is in the sights. The sights on the original flintlocks were German silver or brass, and V-shaped so that a hunter could pull the front sight down into the bottom of the V for split-hair shooting. Jack makes his guns with open, square sights that I am certain are almost as accurate as those of a couple of centuries ago. The .50-caliber iron barrel is so accurate that, shooting offhand at 100 yards, even I can place a group within an eight-inch circle. I'm sure that from a bench rest an expert rifleman could drive a nail with it.

Seated with 120 grains of black powder, the .50-caliber ball leaves the muzzle at 2,200 to 2,300 feet per second and at 100 yards drops only about two inches. Beyond that, the ball loses its flat trajectory rapidly.

You can buy a production-type flintlock for as low as $100, while the finer custom-built guns cost from $250 up.

The flintlock followed the wheel lock of the 18th century and was the rifle that helped to win that expansive portion of our continent west of the Appalachians. The percussion-cap rifle came along about 1807, but for decades after that, the real pioneer passed up the cap and ball for the flintlock, for which he needed only lead, powder, and a piece of flint, quartz, or other suitable rock. Caps, on the other hand, were sometimes lost or damaged, or they failed in crucial moments.

I'm sure the old flintlock also faltered plenty of times, but its essential requirements are so basic that it certainly must have been easier to keep in operation. I learned the hard way that a flintlock could fail in a dramatic moment.

$\mathcal{F}$or its first primitive-weapons hunt, the game department had chosen one of Georgia's wildest mountain areas. When settlers moved into the southern Appalachians one to two centuries ago, this was one of the few regions the homesteaders passed up. There may be a few old house sites and other signs of civilization such as you find throughout the southern Blue Ridge, but neither Jack nor I have ever seen them here.

"Where is our best hunting area?" Jack asked George Speed as we checked in.

"You can almost take your pick," George said. "We don't expect more than 65 or 70 hunters, and they'll be well scattered around these 14,000 acres. Most will hunt the lower ridges and valleys. Anywhere is good. This area is loaded with deer."

From the map, we selected a spot on the headwaters of Sarahs Creek, which flows out of the lofty coves under Rabun Bald, Georgia's second highest mountain, jammed up against the North Carolina line. The steep, rocky logging road into this region practically assured us of isolation.

I don't remember a wetter Sunday afternoon. The weatherman's prediction of possible showers had developed into a steady downpour, and by the time we arrived at the end of the old logging road on Sarahs Creek, fog had closed in so thick that it was difficult to see beyond the front sight of a Kentucky rifle.

We pulled on rainsuits before stepping outside into the drowned woods. We walked along the rim of the logging road until we found a spot level enough to pitch our nine- by 12-foot tent with a 12- by 18-foot tarp in front. After hacking out a 20- by 30-foot clearing, we trimmed enough poles and stakes to hold the canvas in place. With the rain still pouring, we unloaded camp stoves, a portable charcoal grill, our beds, and what groceries we'd need for that evening and the next morning.

It would have been next to impossible to build a fire out in that solid sheet of rain, so after broiling our steaks on the grill under the tarp, we added an armful of green oak and hickory sticks to the charcoal. It made a unique campfire, built in the grill under shelter, but was as comfortable as you could imagine under the circumstances.

We listened to the rain all night and had our coffee an hour before daylight. The gray, soggy dawn found us on the crest of a mountain above camp. Howard elected to watch a little gap where two game trails crossed. With my flintlock cradled in my arm, I walked down the ridge along a game trail that led to a wide oak flat. Jack climbed toward the top of the main ridge, which leveled out into a series of gaps and flats studded with scarlet and northern red oaks loaded with acorns.

*G*ray squirrels were everywhere. I ignored several temptations to bark a squirrel by shooting just below where it lay flat on a limb and letting the explosion of bark kill it. This buck hunting with a primitive firearm was serious business; before we bothered with the grays, we had to have a deer.

I was following the old deer hunter's formula of walking two steps and listening three when I encountered a big buck in the trail. The ridge top was so shrouded in rain and fog that visibility was 50 feet or less, and the buck and I met practically face to face near a thicket.

I guess he was as startled as I, but he recovered first, swapped ends, and disappeared into the buttermilk forest before I could get my sights on him. That was the first time I saw him but not the last.

That afternoon, I climbed the ridge behind camp to look into a few big hollows on either side. I came out on the ridgetop a couple of hundred yards from where I'd met the big buck in the morning fog. After reaching the top, I sat down in a laurel thicket to get my breath and decide whether I should find a stand farther out on the ridge or climb the trail toward the red oak flat on top. The downpour had momentarily slackened to a drizzle.

I think I have a reasonably good game eye, but I never did see this buck walk up. It was almost as if an apparition had appeared before my eyes. I was suddenly aware that the same buck I'd met that morning was framed through the laurel branches less than 50 yards away and was not aware of me.

Almost daintily, be pawed aside a hatful of leaves, and when he put his head down to find an acorn, I slowly raised the rifle. In a sitting position, I braced one elbow on my knee, put the sights on the sweet spot behind his shoulder, and touched off. The flint cracked against the frizzen plate—which is the upright "steel" of the pan cover—as if I'd hit it with a claw hammer. Sparks flew, but that was all.

At the crack, the buck jumped about three feet off the ground and now stood with his front legs slightly apart, looking in my direction. I sat rigid while trying to decide my next move.

With a breech loader, it would have been a simple trick to whang another shell into the chamber and knock down the deer before it went two bounds. Wet powder in a flintlock's pan was another problem.

Either the buck made me out, or a vagrant breeze carried my scent to him. Anyhow he suddenly snorted, whirled, and disappeared.

I looked at the pan. The priming powder was gooey, like wet paint. With a toothpick, I scraped it off the pan and dug it out of the touch-hole, which is the vent connecting pan and barrel. I cleaned and dried the pan with a piece of tissue and put in fresh priming powder, pushing it down into the vent with the toothpick.

I still had no idea whether the gun would fire. At least six gray squirrels were in sight, so I thought I might as well accomplish two things at once—see if the gun would shoot with the dry priming, and bark a squirrel.

The grays around me were either feeding in the high branches, scratching in the leaves, or running through the trees. I waited at least 10 minutes before one finally stopped on an oak limb about 60 feet away. It wasn't lying flat against the limb—the ideal position for barking—but I decided to try it anyway.

Drawing a bead two inches under where the gray was perched, I squeezed the trigger, and the gun blasted off a perfect shot. I must have been aiming a bit too high, though. There was no mark on the tree, and the squirrel simply vanished, as though the .50-caliber ball had picked him up and carried him along on its flight.

Sheltering the barrel of the gun from the drizzle as best I could, I prepared to reload. Measuring out 120 grains of black powder, I poured it into the barrel. Then I seated my bullet in a grease patch and used my short starter to push the bullet down flush with the top of the barrel. I trimmed the patch with my patch knife, used the long starter to push the bullet and patch three inches into the barrel, and then seated them against the powder with the ramrod. I primed the pan with finer powder, closed the frizzen, and set the hammer at half cock.

But this time I didn't leave the lock exposed to weather. I covered it with a dry handkerchief, on top of which I placed a square of aluminum foil from the sandwich in my pack.

If old Dan'l had seen all this, he'd probably have rolled on the ground with laughter.

While this was going on, Jack was having tribulations of his own with a forkhorn higher up on the mountain. More experienced than I, he had covered his lock when he started out that morning and had kept his powder dry.

He was seated in a high cove when the forkhorn and a doe walked by just at the limit of his vision in the fog. He thought they were gone and didn't even slip the cover off his lock. Then the small buck turned and walked straight downhill toward Jack, stopping about 40 feet away and staring directly at him. Very slowly, Jack peeled the cover off his lock and, with almost imperceptible movements, raised his barrel until the sights were right in line with the buck's muzzle.

"I figured I'd either kill clean or miss clean," Jack said later.

In spite of the protection he'd given his powder, the black stuff was damp, and when Jack pulled the trigger, his gun held fire between the flash pan and muzzle blast just long enough to let the buck whirl away. When the smoke cleared, the deer had vanished.

Jack found a few drops of blood, but in a matter of minutes the rain had washed out the sign, and he was unable to trail the animal. He spent three hours looking all over that side of the mountain but was never able to find a trace of the buck. He concluded that the ball had left only a surface wound.

The deer I'd seen was a good eight-pointer, so we decided to concentrate on him for a day. Before dawn, we took stands about 300 yards apart along the high ridge. Freshly rubbed bushes, pawings in the leaves, and assorted tracks showed that the buck and smaller deer had been using there.

We stuck it out through the cold rain that fell all morning. I half expected that the deer had more sense than we did and were bedded down somewhere, but along about 10 o'clock Howard got a cramp in his left leg and reached down cautiously to move his foot to a different angle.

A snort off to his right made him jerk his eyes around in time to see the eight-pointer watching him from the edge of a thicket less than 100 feet away. As Howard felt for his muzzleloader, the big deer whirled and was swallowed by the screen of brush.

When we got back to camp about noon, George Speed and Bob Deal, another ranger, were waiting for us.

"We thought we'd better check to see if you were drowned," George said, "and to bring a bit of news."

They told us that although 65 hunters had checked in, the continuous rain had discouraged all but 21. Four deer had been killed—three does and one spike buck. We told the two officers about the big buck we'd been after.

"Why don't you let him rest," Bob suggested, "and look over some territory George and I found over on Hood Creek. The road between the creek and top of the mountain is full of fresh tracks. In little more than a mile, we found forty-two places where deer had crossed the road. One of those tracks, about two-thirds of the way up the mountain, was made by a buck that must haul a pretty good rack around with him."

"That country has some steep, slick hills," George added, "so we'll take you in with the four-wheel-drive. You can come out without any trouble since it's downhill most of the way."

The rain had let up some when we arrived at the plank bridge over one fork of Hood Creek. Howard turned back toward a flat ridge that paralleled the creek, and Jack and I walked slowly up the road in swirling clouds and mist. As the rangers had said, tracks were all over the place. But I hunted the road to the top of the ridge—where I ran into another downpour—and turned back without glimpsing a deer.

Jack and I spent a second full day in Hood Creek watershed. In the fog, we walked to within 50 feet of a big turkey gobbler, its feathers spread out to shed some of the rain. We stood and watched the bird for a good 10 minutes before it finally made us out, dropped its feathers, and sprinted off into the wet woods.

"If the season were in," Jack said, "we'd have roast turkey tomorrow."

I was standing on top of the mountain when a small doe walked almost over me and on past without ever knowing I was there. The shot was easy, and I had already made up my mind to down the first deer that stepped within range. But when I put the sights on her, my mind went back to the big buck on the ridge above camp, and I couldn't pull the trigger.

Jack found where two bucks had pushed one another around. The sign was fresh, but he didn't see the animals. There seemed to be plenty of deer on Hood Creek, but somehow we could not seem to get a single buck under the sights of our muzzleloaders.

Wednesday night the wind blew, and we woke before daylight on Thursday to a sky full of stars. It was the first time we saw the sky that week.

"They ought to be stirring after that bad weather," I suggested. "Let's get back to our big buck up on the hill. We know at least where he is and what he looks like."

*T*hursday was our first day of a real frontier hunt. It was my idea that we dress in buckskins—mostly for pictures—and pack along a lunch of jerky and parched corn, a staple diet in frontier days. One reason we had passed up buckskins in the rain is that they absorb water like a sponge. When worn by a hunter on the move, they retain body heat very well when wet, but in cold weather on a stand, they can get mighty uncomfortable.

We spread out for half a mile along the ridge top and settled down to wait. The sky brightened, and the big mountain behind me lighted up gradually with the gold of the early morning sun, which finally soared into the blue sky, warming my hands and cheeks.

Squirrels were all over the place. In the carpet of leaves, which were beginning to dry, each squirrel sounded like a herd of whitetails moving in my direction.

I stayed glued in that one spot for some four hours and was beginning to feel as if I were taking root. In spite of my intentions to remain there throughout the day, I was growing a mite restless and was seriously considering a climb up the tall ridge that led toward Rabun Bald when a movement caught my attention. A spot of tan moved in the brush, and the buck stepped into the open not more than 30 yards away. He stood for a long minute, testing the wind and looking up and down the ridge. Then he began to search the forest floor for acorns. I waited until his head went out of sight behind a log before I raised my flintlock and put the sights behind his shoulder.

He was standing broadside, as nearly perfect a shot as I ever hope to have at a deer. When I clicked the hammer back, the buck looked up but did not move. I squeezed the trigger, but nothing happened. I squeezed harder until I knew the trigger would bend under the pressure, but the flint cock was frozen in its position. I tried to work it back and forth with my thumb, but the hammer refused to budge. I clamped down on the trigger again until I was sure it would break off; then I sat helpless and exasperated while the buck fed along the ridge toward Howard.

For another hour after that, I waited for my partner's shot. Then Howard himself appeared, walking stealthily along the game trail on the crest of the ridge. I gave a low whistle, and he angled over.

"The critter fed past me," he said, "but he was down over the side of the ridge, and all I got was one glimpse—not enough for a sure shot."

I told him my sad story, and he looked at my muzzleloader. The flint cock was still frozen in place.

"I'd sure have lost my scalp," I said, "if that buck had been hostile and walking on two legs instead of four."

Back in camp, Jack took my muzzleloader apart. In those four days of rain, the new stock had swelled just enough to lock one of the pins in the mechanism. The piece could be cocked with difficulty but could not be released by trigger pressure. Jack chipped out the offending bulge of wood and oiled the metal parts, and the gun was in perfect working order again.

"What did the old-timers do?" I asked. "Carry gunsmiths with them?"

"I guess a man had to be a pretty good mechanic on his own to stay alive," Jack said.

Farther up the ridge on Friday, I could have killed a doe. For at least five minutes, she fed less than 100 yards away. I was tempted but couldn't quite bring myself to give the flintlock a chance at this plump bit of camp meat. I'm sure that this area is so full of deer that the does need thinning out, but I was more interested in a picture of a good buck than in venison on the table.

Saturday was the last day of the primitive-weapons hunt. The rangers who came up for steaks with us on Friday evening said that only eight deer had been checked so far.

On Saturday, we decided to split up. Since the buck we were after was seen every time within 100 yards of the same spot, we decided that one of us should work that area and the other two fan out in another direction. Since Jack was the best hunter in our group, we assigned him and his flintlock to the ridge above camp. Howard, who was hunting with a cap-and-ball rifle, selected a big cove in which he had discovered abundant sign a few days before. I climbed the steep ridge above an old mica mine a mile or so up the creek from camp. We agreed to meet at camp around noon, pack up, hunt out the remainder of the day, and drive home after dark.

I had a rather exciting day on the ridge I'd chosen. It rose abruptly from the forks of the creek, climbed for half a mile, then leveled off into a long, sloping flat studded with big, acorn-laden oaks. Moving a step or two at a time, into the wind, I jumped four deer. I saw only one—a doe I put my sights on and might have killed—but the shot would have been a quick one, and I passed it up.

One big-bodied animal danced out of the thickets ahead of me and stopped on the side of the hill, but try as I might, I could never make out its outline through the heavy foliage.

I sat in three likely spots for about an hour each, then hunted slowly back down the ridge and got to camp around noon.

Howard arrived a few minutes after I did and reported that he'd passed up a small doe. Thirty minutes later, Jack came in, grinning like a mule fresh out of some brier patch, and dropped his loaded liver sack on the table.

"I guess that critter's luck ran out," he said, "just about the time mine began."

Jack had spent all morning on the ridge top without seeing a deer. An hour before noon, he left his stand to hunt toward camp. He was tiptoeing along the top of the divide when he spooked several deer out of a thicket. One of them was the big buck Howard and I had seen several times.

The south side of the ridge dropped off into a wide, flat hollow. On an impulse, Jack sat down against the huge butt of a white oak where he could watch the hollow for a few minutes before heading down the mountain.

He heard a noise in the leaves off to his left, and as he looked, a doe broke out of the screen of brush and streaked across the hollow about 60 yards below him. He had put up his rifle before identifying her as a doe, so when the big buck bounded into the opening after the doe, he was ready. The eight-pointer paused just long enough for Jack to drill it between the shoulder blades, breaking its back.

He field-dressed it where it lay and came to camp for help in dragging it out to the logging road and camp.

Though Howard and I didn't connect, we were as pleased as Jack was over the kill. Jack magnanimously agreed with us that it was team effort that paid off on the last half day of our hunt.

This primitive-weapons hunt, Jack told me, was initiated by his department to help change the old concept of quantity hunting—or getting as much game as possible by any legal method—to the newer one of quality hunting, in which the pleasure of the hunt is more important than the mere killing of an animal. This was part of the commission's long-range plan to cope with the mounting pressure on game resources.

It convinced us. Even before taking down our tent and packing the gear, we shook hands and made a solemn pledge—to be somewhere in the Warwoman area the next year when muzzleloader time came around again. ◆

From Outdoor Life, *March 1967*

The Canoe Deer

by Erwin A. Bauer

◆

I WAS PUSHING through an evergreen jungle on my hands and knees. The Scotch pines, planted in neat rows by foresters years before, were now crowding together so that I had to crawl like an infantryman under fire.

As I squirmed past a small patch of snow, I saw something a few inches from my face that made my hackles rise—the tracks of a tremendous deer. They were steaming fresh.

Then, maybe 30 feet ahead, I saw legs. I froze in place, and couldn't see any more of the animal until it moved. The deer stepped into a tiny opening. It was a buck with the kind of rack that makes deer hunters feel weak all over.

I tried to inch forward for an unobstructed shot. That slight motion did it. A small twig cracked and the buck bolted. I jumped up and took a snap shot through the only possible opening. I thought the buck stumbled when I fired, but he went on at high speed. I couldn't find a drop of blood along his trail.

Frank Sayers came running toward me. He'd heard me shoot, and the deer had crashed through the pines very close to him. The growth was so thick Frank couldn't see the critter, let alone shoot at it.

"It was a buck—and a dandy, too," I told him. "He was only 30 feet away when I spooked him."

This was my dismal start with Ohio's first state-wide deer season in my lifetime. Previous hunts had been held in selected counties and districts, but this shotgun hunt, opening December 12, 1956, marked the first time in more than 50 years that hunters could try for deer all over the state. Ohio game men figured we had 40,000 deer in '56, which is quite a herd when you consider that wild whitetails were officially extinct in this state in 1911.

Both Frank and I live in Columbus, and we know the Ohio deer herds well. We first considered a hunt in a county in northeastern Ohio, where deer had been hunted only once before in recent times. Deer were abundant there, but perhaps deer hunters would be even more plentiful. We thought about a hunt near home in central Ohio, where the deer feed in alfalfa and cornfields, and grow racks that flirt with Boone & Crockett Club records. But these corn-fed whitetails are very widely scattered. We finally chose the Muskingum country in eastern Ohio. Deer are numerous enough here, big enough—and so hard to hunt in places that many hunters shun the whole region. We picked the Muskingum area because Frank had a theory about how to beat the game.

We set up a simple camp the day before the season opened. Our tent was pitched near the inlet to one of the Muskingum lakes. The equipment we brought to camp was rather unusual for deer hunting, a canoe and a pair of shotguns being the vital items. Shotguns were the only legal firearms during this four-day buck-or-doe season.

Ohio lawmakers have correctly concluded that a shotgun firing a single slug or ball is much safer than a long-range rifle in a generally flat state that's heavily populated.

*T*o understand how we planned to use the canoe on this hunt, you need to know something about the Muskingum country. In 1913, a tragic flood hit this area. Towns like Zanesville were almost obliterated, the toll in lives exceeded 500, and the loss of property ran into hundreds of millions of dollars.

After the flood the Muskingum Watershed Conservancy District was formed by an act of legislature. Large headwater dams were thrown across the more troublesome streams to hold back flood waters. Today there's 16,000 acres of topnotch fishing waters behind those dams, and 365 miles of rugged, almost undisturbed, shoreline. Vast tracts of the flood-ravaged land were planted to trees, mostly evergreens.

All this was fine for an expanding deer herd, and now it ranks with the best whitetail range in the Midwest. But few places are more difficult to hunt. A hunter walking into the dense evergreens is blocked and befuddled like an ant in a thriving lawn. When he breaks out of the thicket he's often blocked by a lake or inlet.

Frank thought a canoe was the answer. We'd travel by water as much as possible, first to find the best patches of cover without tramping through them. Later we could travel to those places quietly and quickly and set up drives.

Ohio's deer season doesn't begin until 9 A.M., and at the stroke of that hour we pushed off for a narrow peninsula on the opposite side of the lake. Much of the peninsula was planted with pines, and the day before we'd seen several deer trails going into it. The plan was to leave Frank on one side of the pines and then paddle around to the opposite side. We'd both hunt slowly toward a point in the center. It worked fine, too. We ran into the big buck on our first drive.

As we sat down to smoke and plan our next move, Frank said, "That buck you just jumped won't go far. The best cover is close to the lake, and other hunters are working the hills."

"Sounds reasonable," I said, "But it will be hard to get another crack at him in this stuff."

"Maybe not," Frank answered. He scraped the pine needles away to clear a patch of bare earth and drew a crescent-shape figure with a dry twig.

"Most of the pine plantings," Frank continued, "are shaped like this—around the contour of the slope. One of us can take a stand on one end, but out in the open, while the other paddles to the opposite side and drives completely through the plantation. We can take turns driving. Maybe that way we can push a deer into the open—or at least to where a man can shoot."

The strategy, again, was sound enough, but our luck was bad. Frank chased out three deer before quitting time—a large doe and a pair of yearlings. But they were out of shotgun range as they passed my stand. The best killing range for the rifled slug in a 12-gauge gun is less than 75 yards. It hits harder at 50 yards than a .30/30 rifle bullet does at 100 yards, but the slug quickly loses accuracy and killing power after 50 yards.

Next morning we started using the same system. It was my turn to make the first stand.

I watched and waited, afraid that my frosted breath might give me away. After several hushed minutes an object moved. It was a big buck. There was no way to be sure, but I thought it was the same one I'd seen before.

I waited, hoping for a clear shot, as the deer stepped behind a screen of pines just to the right. For an age, it seemed, I waited for the deer to show again. Nothing. I was satisfied he'd bedded down right there.

I'd just about decided to make a move to one side to try for a shot when a twig snapped in the pines where the buck had vanished. A second later Frank walked out of the clump I was watching so intently. The buck, instead of bedding down, had completely evaporated, it seemed.

I told Frank how the buck had been moving ahead of him and disappeared. The answer was evident. The deer had turned to the right and sneaked up a small wooded hollow. I felt pretty low. You rarely get a second chance at a fine animal like that.

We pushed off in the canoe to try driving another area. I dropped Frank off on the shore of a small bay. He planned to make a stand near the ruins of a long-abandoned farm building a short distance inland.

I paddled along the shoreline for perhaps half a mile, stopping once to watch for running deer after I heard a barrage of shooting over the hill. At last I turned into another small bay where an old country road led into the water.

Neither of us saw anything until late afternoon. Then, as I finished a long push around a pine hillside just before dusk, Frank hailed me excitedly.

"You ran two deer out of that place," he told me. "A small doe took off for the next county, but that buck, or his twin brother, sneaked back into the same pines where you first jumped him."

"But it's too late for another drive," I said.

"I know," Frank agreed, "but I have a hunch the buck will stay in those pines till morning. I could see the whole area from up here, and he didn't come out the other side. I think the pines are his favorite hide-out."

J was doubtful about it, but agreed to drive the pines next morning.

Frank had a pot of coffee boiling long before shooting time next morning. It was still dark when I crawled out of the sleeping bag to join him. We put in a couple of hours drinking coffee and puttering around camp before 9 o'clock, the legal shooting hour.

The pine plantation where Frank figured the buck would still be hanging out was perfect for our two-man system. It was dense inside but fairly open all around. It was roughly triangular in shape, and a deer just might be driven out through one point, especially through the corner that was close to another mass of cover. We decided that Frank should take a stand at that corner while I worked in his direction.

I pushed headlong into the dense evergreens without any attempt to move quietly. Once I drifted too far toward one edge and could see the sedge border. I was cutting back again when a deer went crashing out ahead of me.

As I smashed out to the edge of the thicket, Frank's gun boomed. I saw the deer running through the clearing ahead of me. It stumbled, regained its feet, and disappeared over a low rise. I followed and found the animal dead 100 feet farther on. It was a beautiful white-tail buck, a typically big Ohio eight-pointer. Frank had plunked a slug into him squarely amidships. I called out and held its head up as Frank came running.

Frank Sayers has bagged many a whitetail in many a different place, but I'm sure none gave him as great a thrill as this trophy he collected not far from home. We were preparing to dress the animal when he said, "Looks like you had a hand in bagging this deer, too."

"I'll admit I didn't do a bad job of driving," I said.

"More than that," Frank answered. "Look at this back leg."

The bone was broken several inches from the ground, the hoof hanging loosely by a tendon. Probably the result of my hurried shot that first day.

Finally, on the last day, my aim was much better. But next to Frank's deer it was little more than a consolation prize. Yet it saved me a woolen shirttail, which is the penalty paid in our camps by the hunter who has chances but fails to connect.

Getting Frank's deer across the lake to camp was no easy matter. Just try to load a 200-pound deer into a 13-foot canvas canoe and you'll see what I mean. A dead deer is limp all over. To make it worse, loading the critter was a one-man job because my canoe couldn't handle Frank and me—total weight 450 pounds—and the deer as well. So first I shuttled Frank to camp and then returned for the deer alone.

Even my smaller deer was a problem to move. Just to reach my canoe, I had to drag the animal half a mile uphill, then carry it across a knee-deep, ice-cold feeder creek.

That's why, in camp that night, I insisted on the bigger portion of the fried deer liver. ◆

From Outdoor Life, *October 1957*

Whitetails Make Mistakes

by Ben East

They're not in the habit of acting like fools. But if you hunt slowly and give a deer a chance to goof, you might hang him on the meat pole.

———————◆———————

I'VE BEEN HUNTING DEER FOR close to 40 years, and I can count on my fingers the rack-carrying whitetails I have encountered in that time that have made downright foolish mistakes. Nevertheless, it does happen.

A few falls back, my friend Jess Furbush left his northern Michigan camp one morning in a wet snowstorm and walked out along an old logging road on his way to a stand. Passing through a patch of hardwood, he heard the groaning, creaking sound of two trees rubbing together a few yards to his right. That's a common noise in the woods, however, and Jess gave it little thought.

As he shuffled along a quarter of a mile farther down the trail, rifle cradled in his left arm and the hood of his parka pulled up over his head, he heard precisely the same sound, again in the woods on his right.

It struck him as queer that there should be two pairs of trees rubbing together so close to the logging road and such a short distance apart. He looked around, and there, only 15 feet away and uttering low, moaning bleats as it walked, was a buck moving through the timber on a course parallel to his own.

Jess stopped abruptly. The deer did the same, and the two of them stood there staring at each other through the falling snow.

Jess reasoned that if he tried to switch the rifle to his right hand, bring it to his shoulder, and turn halfway around for a shot, the deer would be gone before he could kill it.

So instead, he just let the rifle slide into his hands, swung it across in front of him without lifting it more than a few inches, and cut loose a left-handed shot from the hip. The deer went down as if sledged and stayed where it fell. Jess still has trouble getting people to believe the story.

Such behavior is anything but typical, of course. The whitetail buck is one of the wariest and craftiest game animals in the woodlands of North America, superbly equipped, and not much given to making a fool of himself.

He has fairly sharp eyesight, keen hearing, and a nose as good as they come. He's also smart, with inborn cunning and wisdom gained by hard experience. He takes advantage of the wind and cover, watches where he's going, keeps an eye on his back track, does his level best to stay out of danger. Cornered in a spot where every avenue of escape is blocked and he must expose himself if he runs, he has the nerve and common sense to lie doggo, head stretched out flat on the ground, not batting an eye. He'll let a hunter walk past 10 paces away and never move until the coast is clear. Or he'll sneak out as quietly as a cat on a velvet rug, crouched low and moving like a shadow.

As a youngster, he may be as short on caution as a farmyard calf. It's a common experience for fawns to walk up and look men over, bursting with curiosity and itching to get acquainted. A hunter I know, sitting on a stump at the edge of thick stuff a couple of falls ago, watched a button buck saunter in, size him up, step closer, and actually sniff at his glove. One sniff was enough. That foolish little deer lit out as if the woods had caught fire, making jumps three times his own length.

Don't expect older whitetails to behave that way. The buck soon outgrows his fawnhood innocence. If he survives through his second or third fall, he has learned most of what he needs to know, but he'll go right on getting smarter as long as he lives.

For all his craft and wisdom, however, he's not infallible, as hunters sometimes are tempted to believe. If he were, venison would be scarce. Fundamentally, every deer hunt is a contest of wits, and there can be only two outcomes. Either the deer or the hunter wins. Usually the loser loses because he did something wrong, and a fair share of the time it's the deer that goofs. It may not be a big mistake. Not once in a lifetime can you expect a whitetail to shadow you and ask to be killed, as the one did that Jess shot in the snowstorm. But if you are hunting the way you should, a small error on the deer's part is all it takes to put you ahead.

Whitetail eyesight is only fair where motionless objects are concerned, and apparently deer either don't see or don't pay much attention to strange color in the landscape, such as a splotch of red or yellow hunting clothing. But they have eyes like a hawk's for anything that moves. I've come over a ridge, lifted just my cap brim into view on the skyline, and spooked a feeding buck 75 yards away.

All the same, I once gathered in a good buck for no better reason than that he failed to keep his eyes open when he and I were both out for a walk.

It was the first morning of deer season on Beaver Island, off the Michigan mainland in northern Lake Michigan. I picked a stand at the edge of an abandoned farm where deer had been feeding on apples in the old orchard, and the runways showed plenty of use.

About an hour after daylight an eight-pointer came out of the brush on the far side of the clearing, too far away for shooting, and trotted 100 yards in plain view. Something had spooked him, for he kept looking back the way he had come. Finally he cut across the upper end of the clearing toward a swamp, still too far away for me to reach. He had almost gained cover when another hunter, whose presence I had known nothing about, piled him up at easy range. I was as surprised as the deer.

The man's partner came along, and the two of them started to dress the kill. They hadn't been at it five minutes when a second buck broke out of the swamp and started across the clearing 50 yards from them, going at a hard run. The partner took care of that one in short order. Both deer had made the mistake of exposing themselves in the open in full daylight with hunters in the woods all around them. Maybe the fact that it was the opening morning of the season had something to do with their behavior. Whitetails grow less wary when there's no shooting.

Anyway, with two bucks killed from the same stand in less than 10 minutes, I decided I'd better move to another spot. I didn't bother to hunt as I went, for I figured any deer in that neighborhood had been driven out by the shooting. It was a dry, warm morning with a good breeze blowing, and the woods were noisy. Dead leaves crackled underfoot, but I made no effort to be careful.

Yet, before I had walked 300 yards into the timber, I saw something move off to my right. It was a buck moseying along between the trees on a course that would have brought the two of us together in another minute or so. The wind was wrong for him to get my scent, and I suppose he was too far away to hear me walk, but all he needed to do was take one look in my direction to make me out. He didn't, and I saw him first. I stopped, put the front sight of my rifle on an open place between two tree trunks, and waited for him to walk into it. He never knew what hit him.

A deer's ears are hard to match. He knows every natural noise in woods and sorts out foreign sounds in a hurry, especially a human voice, even speaking in an undertone. I once watched a buck sneaking off along the border of a swamp ahead of two greenhorns who were conversing in a low mumble. They were 200 yards away, out of sight in thick stuff. The deer, flattened down with his belly almost to the ground and his head low, was keeping the pair located as if he were tracking them by radar. The mistake he made was in ignoring that I might be up on the ridge overlooking his get-away route, which I was.

Sharp as a deer's hearing is, it lets him down every now and then on one vital score. He fails to locate the source of a sound, even a loud sound close by, and either moves the wrong way or fails to move at all until it's too late.

Several years ago I was sitting at the side of an old logging road in northern Michigan one morning, watching a runway that came angling out of a steep ravine and crossed about 60 paces to my left. The road wound through open timber, but the runway was partly screened by young hemlocks and I couldn't see a deer coming up the hill until it stepped into the open.

I had reached the place an hour after daylight. The earth was wet from a night of cold November rain, so I cut an armful of hemlock branches to sit on. I didn't expect anything to happen right after that for, in gathering the boughs, I had made enough noise by my own reckoning to spook any deer within hearing. Yet within three or four minutes after I had settled down, a deer stepped out of the hemlocks at the spot where the runway crossed the road.

It halted just at the edge of the brush. Michigan had a buck law at the time, and I was carrying a .300 Savage with no scope and couldn't make out antlers. I did have a pair of 7X binoculars buttoned inside the front of my shirt, however, and when I got them out and leveled, I was looking at a nice eight-pointer.

While I was tucking the glasses back out of the way, he walked across the road, and by the time I was ready to shoot, his head was hidden in thick stuff. I could still see his shoulder and the rest of him back of it, but there was a thicket of young maple whips no bigger than a man's thumb at the side of the road between me and the deer.

I sized the situation up and took plenty of time. The buck's hind-quarters were in the open, free of brush, but I didn't want to shoot him there. Only a few times in all my hunting have I had to trail a wounded deer. It's an unpleasant chore, and to avoid it I like to put my shots ahead of the diaphragm if I can. In this case I decided on the shoulder, despite the fact that it was partly screened by brush.

I braced my elbow on my left knee, pulled the gold bead down into the crotch of the rear sight and centered it on a tan patch of deer. I was steady as a rock and as sure of the buck as if he were already hanging on the meat pole back at camp.

The rifle smashed out its sharp report, but nothing else happened. The deer neither fell, flinched, nor moved. I waited a second for him to go down, then racked in another shell and tried again for the same spot.

It's hard to believe, but I fired three cool, deliberate shots at that buck standing broadside 60 yards away, and they had no more effect than if I'd been shooting blanks.

It wasn't the fault of the rifle, the sights, or me. Brush deflected my 180-grain bullets three times in a row, and the deer simply stood there, waiting to make sure where the noise was coming from before he moved. It was a disconcerting experience. When I racked the fourth cartridge into the chamber, the clatter of the action finally gave me away. The buck swapped ends and was back in the hemlocks in two lightning jumps, and I threw my fourth shot away as he went out of sight. That was as good an example as I've ever heard about of a deer waiting until he is certain in which direction danger lies before he jumps.

One thing deer, even young or reckless ones, can't tolerate is human scent. Back around 1930 I spent a couple of weeks in midsummer photographing whitetails at a fire lookout's cabin miles back in the woods on the Tahquamenon River in Michigan's upper peninsula. There was a sizable clearing around the cabin grown tall with timothy and wild grass, and all through the summer, 30 to 40 deer pastured in that clearing.

It was not in a park or refuge, but for some reason those whitetails were the least wary lot I have ever had anything to do with. The tamest of the herd was an old doe that showed little more respect for a man than for another deer—which wasn't much.

I took pictures of her until I tired of it. I could walk up within 10 feet of her in the open and without making the slightest effort at stalking or concealing myself. But I had to keep the wind in my favor. Every so often she'd grow suspicious and work around where she could get my scent, and that ended our beautiful friendship every time. The instant she smelled me she'd cut loose with a terrific snort, panic all the others, throw up her flag, run at top speed for 100 feet or so, then stop and look back with a foolish expression on her face as if wondering why she had lost her head. Thirty seconds later she'd be feeding again, but it would take the rest of the bunch at least half an hour to screw up enough courage to work their way cautiously back into the clearing. That old girl wasn't really afraid of me. She just couldn't stand the way I smelled.

When a whitetail's nose tells him there's a man in the area, he's almost sure to pay attention. Yet there are exceptions even to that rule. On a hunt in northern Wisconsin one time I encountered a buck that ignored that warning.

He came into sight from an unexpected quarter, 250 yards downwind from my stand. It was too long a shot for iron sights, and although he was moving toward me, I wrote him off, knowing he'd get my scent long before he was within range. But to my surprise he kept coming through thick brush. I caught glimpses of him now and then but had no chance for a good shot until he was about 40 yards off. Then, although he came into the open, he continued walking straight for me, I held my fire to see what would happen.

He couldn't possibly have failed to smell me, yet he marched up to within 30 feet before he stopped behind some small evergreens and looked over them as if he wanted to play peekaboo. I decided the flirtation had gone far enough.

Over most of his range—and he's found in just about every state, except Alaska and Hawaii, as well as in Mexico and all through southern Canada—the whitetail is a deer of brush and thickets. He can, however, make out in country with sparse cover if he has to. Whitetail hunting is at least as good in the prairie counties of the Dakotas as in the Black Hills, for example, and Iowa, not a heavily timbered state, yielded 4,000 whitetails to 8,000 hunters in the fall of 1961, a very good average.

In general, though, this deer prefers thick cover. Where it's available, he stays in it, especially after the shooting starts. Most of the deer killed in the eastern half of the country are dropped in, or not far from the edge of, brush or timber. They rarely venture out into the open in hunting season.

Yet, by way of demonstrating the whitetail weakness for making a fatal mistake now and then, one of the nicest bucks I ever took was shot in the middle of Sleeping Bear dune, a mountain of shifting sand on the shore of Lake Michigan, 30 miles west of Traverse City, Mich.

Except for patches of dune grass and sand cherry, and a few sparse islands of aspen in the wind-scooped hollows, that big dune is as open as a true desert. Five miles long and two wide, it has neither food nor water, and there is no good reason for deer to cross it. Yet they wander all over it, leaving their tracks in the sand through spring, summer, and fall.

Hidden in a thin clump of aspens, a companion and I watched that particular buck come at a walk for half a mile before he got close enough for a shot. The time was around noon, the season was a week old, and the surrounding swamps and timber had been hunted hard. He had no business being there at all. The dune produced three or four good bucks in that same fashion in the two falls I hunted there, when the county was first thrown open to deer hunting around 1940.

What's the best way for a hunter to cash in on whitetail mistakes? Is there a method of hunting that's likely to tip the scales in your favor consistently when the deer blunders? There is, and the formula is a simple one: hunt slowly and be alert.

As a matter of fact, any list of deer-hunting rules I ever compile will have that one at the top. It has accounted for most of the venison I have brought home, and most of the chances I have missed were botched because I broke it.

I'm not talking here about runway watching. That accounts for a lot of deer and I do my share of it, in small doses, though, since I lack the patience for long periods on a stand, especially in cold weather. When I say hunt slowly, the tip is intended for the hunter who is on the move.

The surest way to score is to take plenty of time. Walk one step and stand still two, an old-timer told me more than 30 years ago. Nobody ever gave me better advice. The more slowly you move the less likely a deer is to see you first. Make frequent stops, and look over every foot of the country ahead before you go on. If you come to the top of a hill or the edge of a clearing, make sure there are no deer in sight before you show yourself. Then wait a little longer on the chance you may have overlooked something. If there's a whitetail around, let him move first.

You have to give the deer an opportunity to do something wrong. Maybe he'll be sneaking or running from another hunter and will blunder into you. Maybe he'll show himself at the edge of a thicket. If he's bedded down, he may fail to smell or hear you until it's too late (you're wasting your time stillhunting unless you watch the wind), or he may wait too long before he slams out. Don't hurry. Give him a chance to goof.

It pays to watch your back track, too. Deer are likely to leave cover after you have gone past, or wander along behind you by accident. I once killed a nice six-pointer in the Canadian border country of northern Minnesota by waiting at the edge of a swamp after it had been driven and the drivers had moved on. The buck circled around them safely but made the mistake of trying to get back into his home thickets 15 minutes later.

That's deer hunting. Stop and wait in the right place and you get your chance. Let impatience get the upper hand, walk too fast or move too soon, and the deer wins.

Hunting at a leisurely pace, however, won't fill the meat pole by itself. It takes alertness as well as patience to do that. Much of the time, especially on bare ground, you have no advance warning of the deer's presence. He may be standing in brush just ahead, or lying in the top of a windfall 20 yards to one side, but you have no way of knowing that. So there's only one thing to do: hunt every minute as if you expect him behind the next bush, over every rise, at the bottom of each ravine. Maybe he'll be there, maybe he won't, but you can't afford to drop your guard.

*E*xpect the unexpected. Keep your eyes open, your ears cocked. When you stop, don't just stand. Look and listen, hard. If there's a wind blowing in puffs, move when it blows, listen when it dies away. And remember that the less commotion you make, the greater the odds in your favor. A walk in the woods for exercise is one thing, a deer hunt is another. The most stupid whitetail you'll ever meet (and you won't meet many) can get the best of you if you're not doing your part.

Not one hunter in 1,000 will ever match the experience two friends of mine had in Minnesota some years ago. Our party arrived in camp a day or two before the season opened, always a good idea, and this pair went out without guns to scout for sign and stands. Following a runway, they saw a huge 12-point buck come around a bend in the trail 50 yards away headed straight for them with his nose to the ground as if he were smelling a doe track.

The men stopped, but the deer came on, taking no notice of them until he was only six or seven paces away. He pulled up short then, stiffened like a dog on point, shook his head, and started to paw the ground like an enraged bull.

He pawed and bluffed for a couple of minutes, showing no fear at all. Then he stood for another minute or two, motionless and rigid, staring angrily at the men. At last he backed off the runway, sneaked sideways a few yards into the brush, and crashed away.

That happened during the rut, and deer aren't always in their right minds then. Don't look for it to happen to you. Whitetails rarely make such stupid and dangerous blunders.

The canniest of them, though, are guilty of small errors. If you are ready when it happens, even a trifling whitetail mistake can put venison in your freezer or a rack on your wall.

From Outdoor Life, *December 1962*

Homecoming Buck Hunt

by Byron W. Dalrymple

The hazard in hunting with my sons, I discover, is that they sometimes get the idea that they know just as much as I do.

THE BUCK WAS A STARTLING SIGHT. I pressed close behind a small clump of bushes, the only hiding spot I'd been able to find when I first saw him. Shaking, I was trying to judge the spread of his antlers. Surely they'd go 26 inches, and for a whitetail that is a trophy rack. It proved once again that in the Hill Country of south-central Texas, where white-tails swarm but are mostly of modest size, you can find some old busters if you keep looking.

It wasn't that I especially wanted a record-book deer. But I did want a big one and had promised myself that this year (1968) I'd settle for nothing else. I knew precisely the sort of head I was after. Texas is a huge state with strikingly varied terrain. Its deer, too, vary greatly from place to place. For several years I'd been trying to collect a really big, prime 10-pointer with heavy dark-mahogany-colored antlers.

Now I was watching a big buck move across a completely open area. The temptation to shoot instantly was all but uncontrollable. The buck was following a doe, his attention completely focused on her. I was uncomfortably close, but not a breath of breeze was stirring. With great care I studied the animal.

The thought suddenly hit me that I knew of nowhere else in the entire U.S. that a hunter could see a sight exactly like this. A short distance behind the buck was a woven-wire fence 10 feet high. Not to fence deer in, but rather to fence them out.

Over large portions of the Edwards Plateau, or Hill Country, of Texas you can see many of these fences. There are so many whitetails that crops can't grow without deerproof fences. Long stretches of highway have such fences on either side because of the unusual danger to traffic from swarming deer. At least 15,000 Texas deer were killed on highways alone last year—more than are killed by hunters in at least 18 other states.

Where I live, a few miles out in the country, we can't grow flowers or a vegetable garden. Deer eat everything. On opening morning of the season I had peered out my bedroom window and seen seven, a modest buck among them, lying in the yard at dawn.

Now the old buster I'd been watching from behind the bushes moved ahead in a short spurt and put his nose down to the track of the doe. Gingerly I eased up my camera instead of my gun and took his picture. As I snapped the shutter he was pawing the ground. My movement alerted him. He jerked up his head and stared. I eased the camera to the ground, gripped my .243 Winchester Model 70, and debated about shooting.

"What a fool!" I thought after deciding to pass him up. "I know I'll regret it. I'll probably never get another chance like this." Handsome and big as that buck was, his antlers were almost white, as if he had reached and just passed his prime.

I stayed still until the buck moved out of sight. Then I arose, still shaking, and went to find Terry, my younger son. He was at the four-wheel-drive rig when I got there. He'd not had a shot.

"Terry," I said, "I'd have given anything if you'd been in my place. What a buck! But not exactly what I wanted."

About then Mike, my older boy, came in. As I told the story both boys groaned. I didn't blame them.

This was a very special hunt for us, a kind of homecoming buck hunt in December during the Christmas holidays, a hunt we'd thought would never come off. Terry, 14 then, had for the first time in his life done a stint in the hospital. Mike, at 18, had gone off for his first year in college. I'm an outdoor writer and had been away most of the fall on magazine assignments.

The three of us, since the boys were small, have been a rather close-knit trio, often fishing or hunting together. But the fall of '68 was a kind of family break-up time. It had seemed that, for the first time, we'd have to forgo what we all eagerly looked forward to each season, our annual deer hunt. We weren't sure Terry would be up and around in time, Mike didn't think he could get home, and I wasn't sure whether I could.

Then, at the last minute, everything had jelled and the hunt was on.

In the world of deer hunting the state of Texas is a paradox: deer in nuisance numbers, and almost no public lands on which to hunt them. It is estimated by the Texas Parks and Wildlife Department that at least one-fifth of the total U.S. deer herd is within the boundaries of this state, and some real trophies are among them.

In west Texas, desert mule deer are superbly abundant. Brewster County alone produces an average kill of over 5,000 each year during a two-week season. In the south-Texas brush country outsize whitetails with stunning racks of exactly the sort I wanted cruise the cactus patches. Hunters take as many as 3,500 a season out of a typical brush-country county such as Webb, where Laredo is located. In the Hill Country, where I live, a single county may show a harvest of as many as 13,000 whitetails for the season (which, incidentally, for 1969 ran from November 8 to January 1 in most counties). These deer are in general smaller than those in the brush country.

Few hunters go deerless, that's sure. A check of locker plants in my town last fall showed that almost 1,200 deer were brought in during the first three days of the season, and estimates indicated that as many more went home on cars!

However, despite an annual deer kill of about 300,000, Texas has virtually no public deer hunting. You must own your own land, get an invitation from a landowner, lease hunting rights, or pay a fee. Hunt fees run from $50 to $300, depending on what services are furnished. An average package hunt, with guide and transport and often a camp house to stay in, costs about $150. Most such hunts have a three-day time limit, though few hunters need that long to score.

Actually this situation is not something for a hunter to wring his hands over. It is a bargain, since getting a deer is almost surefire and the license is downright cheap: $25 for a nonresident, $3.15 for a resident. This setup allows a hunter to take two whitetail bucks, a bonus doe (by permit from the landowner), and one mule-deer buck—a possible bag of four deer if you have the time, desire, and money.

Chambers of commerce in small cities and towns are the best bet for help in lining up a hunt. Most chambers keep lists of leases and of ranches offering package hunts.

Although I have my own small ranch, the boys and I were hunting that morning on the ranch of a friend. Mike, when he got around to telling his story, was all worked up over a buck he'd seen as it moved into a stand of brush and scrub oak on a distant ridge.

"I bet that buck was going in there to bed down," he said. "I didn't bother him. I figured maybe if you'd both come with me Terry could get him."

"Brotherly love!" I chided.

"Let's go," Terry said. "But it's your buck if we jump him, Mike."

We use what may seem like an odd system when the three of us hunt as a group. We decide who is to do the shooting, and as a rule that person carries the only rifle. The two others go along just to help the shooter. This puts each of us totally on his own and makes the hunt both sporty and safe. We clambered into the vehicle now, and Mike drove to the area in which he had spotted the deer.

"If you and Terry will go slowly along the side of the ridge in plain sight," he said, "I'll sneak in from the other side. If that deer is bedded where I think, he'll see you but he won't get out. If he's watching you, he won't see me. What do you think?"

"Let's try it," I said.

The type of hunting that Mike likes best is sneaking, one step at a time. Mike had previously killed several deer with this technique. There's no better method and none more interesting, and a successful sneak is something to take pride in. But the sneak hunter must learn to go slowly. Mike and I have sometimes spent an hour moving only a few hundred yards. The previous year we had each killed a buck at 10 paces just that way.

"Stay in the open where I can see you," Mike said as we separated.

Terry and I walked slowly, casually, Terry whistling fragments of a tune. After a bit we sat on a rock, surely within sight of any deer bedded atop that ridge a quarter-mile away. I knew about how far Mike had to go, and I kept looking at my watch, trying to visualize his movement and time him. Suddenly Terry squeezed my arm.

"Look!" he said excitedly. "Back in the oaks to our right maybe a hundred yards."

A deer was moving stealthily there one step at a time. I could see antlers. Slowly I raised my binoculars. It was, I guessed, at least an eight-pointer—and a nice one. It peered past a tree trunk, staring at us. Then it turned its head far around as if watching its back trail. That told the story. The deer had not winded Mike, but something the young hunter had done had disturbed it. The buck was not sure which way to go.

"Your darned brother." I mumbled to Terry. "He makes a stalk, and now he doesn't even see the deer."

At that instant the .243 barked, and the sound reverberated off the opposite bluff. The buck made one great bound and took off down the slope.

"He's hit," Terry yelled. "Hard! I saw him stumble."

We leaped up and bolted toward the action. We got to the spot before Mike did. The buck, down for keeps, was a dandy. It was a riot to see Mike come barreling across the ridgetop, leaping bushes, hot on the trail of his wounded buck. When he saw us he slowed down and grinned sheepishly. But there was no need for embarrassment. He'd done a most impressive job.

$\mathcal{T}$hat afternoon I hunted with Terry. He was eager, now that Mike had scored. It was only fair, I felt, to give him a chance and some help before I went back to my trophy hunting. Also, I couldn't get that big deer out of my mind. Maybe I could find the old brute for Terry.

A buck that's in rut and actively following a doe generally has his territory well staked out. He may leave it while chasing a doe. But often the pair will circle round and round in an area of half a mile or so, and a big buck that is glassy-eyed over a doe is commonly a real setup.

Terry and I took a stand in brush on a ridge, and the still day played in our favor. Presently a group of five deer, not an antler in the crowd, passed so close that I had to wait with my telephoto-lens camera until they moved on some distance before I could get them into the frame.

After an hour Terry and I got up and moved carefully along the ridge. Terry spotted a doe and fawn. The fawn had its eye on us; the doe was looking to our left.

"Terry," I whispered, "ease around, and look where that doe is looking. Don't spook the fawn."

Standing there, backlighted but in shadow, was another deer. It had its head down. We could see a bit of antler thrusting past a tree trunk.

"Be ready!" I hissed.

The deer took one step ahead, and I was disappointed. Small.

"You want it?" I asked.

Terry shook his head.

"Good for you," I said. "Let's go get Mister Big."

Deer hunting is almost always full of upsets, exasperations, disappointments. That's what keeps it interesting. Terry and I were about to get "interested."

We sat down beside a hunk of fallen timber, spang in the middle of the area in which I'd seen the big fellow that morning. As if pre-arranged, we heard the racket of a running deer. A doe appeared, loping through the woods. Presently the buck appeared. He was tremendous. I was positive it was the same buck I'd seen earlier.

Terry raised the rifle. There was a small hole to shoot through, but the buck moved. I trained my camera's long lens on the next hole, certain that I was going to get a picture of that monster hitting the ground when Terry fired. The buck appeared in the opening. Then I felt a minor breeze on the back of my neck.

"Oh, no!" I thought.

The buck whirled and stared, its nostrils flaring, and before Terry could fire, it bolted back the way it had come. Terry tried desperately to turn. Ironically, if he had been sitting where I was, the shot would have been wide open. In his spot, however, a tree cut him off.

That buck was, I'm certain, the biggest whitetail that Terry is likely to have a chance at for a long time to come.

"Dang his hide," I blurted. "I wish now I had dropped him this morning."

But that buck was not to be ours. This rancher on whose land we were hunting had other hunters coming for the remainder of the week, so we had to move on. I decided to give both Terry and myself a chance on the noted YO Ranch out of Mountain Home, Texas. Some substantial trophies have been taken there, and Charlie Schreiner, the owner, had been urging us to come out.

"The season's almost over, Dad," Terry said as the boys and I drove on the ranch, with Charlie along to show us around. "No trophy deer for me today. You stay with it if you want to, but the first decent buck that shows is mine."

I went off on my own and glassed several bucks but held my fire. In the afternoon, I went with the others. Charlie spotted what looked like a good buck. Mike stayed with the vehicle, and the rest of us made a stalk. The deer proved to be a very nice eight-pointer. Terry got ready to shoot. The deer stood momentarily, staring, then bounded into a thicket.

"That's that," I muttered. But for some reason this crazy buck turned and started back out of the thicket.

"Shoot it, Terry!" Charlie whispered.

At the same instant, the .243 in Terry's hands cracked. The deer bounded out, ran a few yards, and dropped.

Terry was elated. He was also determined to drag his own deer in.

But that determination didn't last long, and Mike came to his rescue, ribbing him.

We hunted with Charlie for two more days. I kept seeing bucks that I knew I should shoot. This fee-hunt ranch is in the so-called Divide Country, astride the top of the watershed whose western streams flow toward the Rio Grande and whose eastern ones flow toward the Guadalupe River. Some big whitetail bucks roam this region.

Finally, however, the boys and I went down to our own place. While Mike hunted for a doe to be made into sausage and jerky, Terry and I scoured the canyons for a big buck for me. We'd seen three there before the season.

Late in the afternoon the three of us parked the four-wheel-drive in the creek and made a small fire on a flat rock. The ranch was very dry, and we were playing it safe. We hunkered there roasting hunks of backstrap from Mike's deer.

"Dad," Terry said, an evil little glint in his eye, "we know as well as you do what you want. You want to go down to the brush farther south. That's why you won't shoot here. You know darned well some of those you've seen here are big enough. You just think there's a bigger one farther south."

"Oh, come on now," I mumbled.

But by dark that evening I had phoned ahead and made arrangements to hunt a place some distance south. The south-Texas brush country is renowned for its big whitetails, a few of which are in the record book, but they are awfully difficult to hunt in the dense low cactus and thornbrush.

All the way down I was visualizing those big dark antlers—and knowing that this was a precarious undertaking, what with the season ending in two days.

The first day's hunting was typical of how exasperating the brush country can be. Here it was almost New Year's, but hot as summer. Not a deer stirred. A hunter new to this country would think at such times that it had no deer. To a hunter accustomed to seeking whitetails in the woods, the very idea of deer living in such a place is preposterous. Yet the deer are there. Even on good days, however, when the rut is on and the bucks are running, hunting is difficult. A deer can see you for a mile, but often you can't see the deer at short range.

*K*en Shockley, who operates an auto agency in Laredo, had set up this hunt for us. Somehow during that hot late afternoon Ken spotted a good buck and put it on the ground. Though I wanted something still larger, this one got my adrenalin up and wiped out some of the discouragement I was feeling. The antlers were heavy and dark, typical of bucks in this region.

"If only it would turn cold," I complained to Ken.

"You know what they say about Texas weather," he said. "If you don't like it, wait a minute and it'll change."

Sure enough, that evening a whistling norther blew in. I lay in my bunk elated, listening.

"Tomorrow's the day, old father," Mike whispered. "I just feel it."

But as so often happens with weather changes here, behind that norther came a drizzle, and the drizzle became a steady, cold, soaking rain. When it rains like that in south Texas, even four-wheel-drive rigs are easily bogged down.

However, the four of us, swathed in raingear, loaded up. We slid and ground our way in four-wheel drive for an hour, peering out, trying to spot a deer. With dull light and in the drab brush, that is all but impossible. The bulldozed trails got worse and worse. Twice we bogged down and had to get out and gather dead mesquite to put under the wheels.

Suddenly Ken cut off idle gab by jabbing the brakes so hard that we slid sideways down the trail. Then he wheeled wildly in behind a screen of brush.

"Great gods!" he said. "There's a buck sticking his head out of the brush off to our left that's too big to be true! Get out—hurry up!"

I clawed for my rifle. I clawed for cartridges. I clawed at the door.

"How the devil do you open this cussed thing?"

"Tear the door off!" Mike yelled, waving his arms. "Get out. I saw him. Tremendous!"

Somehow I got out. I jammed just one cartridge into the .243. There was little time, I knew. A big buck would not stand still long, not in this country. I eased into the brush ahead of the vehicle, watching which way Ken pointed. Then cautiously I peered through a small opening in the scrub mesquite.

The deer was possibly 125 yards distant, on a small ridge, surrounded by huajillo shrubs. Only its head and a bit of neck showed. It was immobile, staring at the point where the vehicle had disappeared. It was one of the finest whitetails I had ever seen.

I raised the rifle, shaking so badly that I could not hold steady. I pushed off the safety, started to squeeze, then jerked the trigger. There was a metallic click. By great good fortune—that shot would never have connected—in my frenzy I had not jacked the cartridge into the chamber.

"Settle down," I mumbled.

It was inconceivable to me that this huge old buck should give me so much time. The crosshair found his neck. The barrel wavered. Then the shot was away, the report dull in the soggy brush. The deer whirled and was swallowed by the cover.

*T*his time Mike beat me to the spot. No buck was there. But we found ample evidence that the deer had been fatally hit. It lay not 10 yards away, and yet the brush was so dense that we circled several times before finding it—a handsome 10-pointer with heavy dark antlers, exactly what I had hoped for. We were jubilant. Although we did not get a chance to weigh the buck, we estimated that it was well over 200 pounds on the hoof.

All the way home the rain poured down and I stewed about my prize getting soaked atop the car. The boys amused themselves by low-rating my hunting ability and suggesting such things as bringing the wet deer inside and putting it on the seat with me.

"Worst thing is, Mike," Terry said slyly, "when he gets it home, no matter how hard it's raining somebody'll have to hold a hat over a camera and somebody else'll have to take endless pictures of him and his deer."

Which proves that kids often know just as much as their parents. Terry had things doped out just right. ◆

From Outdoor Life, *December 1969*

Jack O'Connor's Last Hunt

by Jack Atcheson, Sr.
as told to Jim Zumbo

When Jack asked whether we could hunt
whitetails together, I was overwhelmed.
Little did I know this would be the legend's
final outing.

◆

T HE WHITETAIL BUCK WAS
enormous, bigger than any I'd ever
seen before. Though I'd hunted
around the world many times, I'd never
been as excited as I was at that moment.
The buck's rack was high and heavy,
with at least 12 points on each side, and
his brow tines were each easily one foot
long. As an official Boone and Crockett
Club measurer, I knew that the deer was
an easy candidate for the record book.

The buck's size wasn't the only reason for my excitement. Jack O'Connor was sitting a few feet away from me, and Jack wanted a big whitetail, bigger than any he'd ever taken.

At the time of our hunt in the fall of 1977, Jack O'Connor was a living legend. Having been OUTDOOR LIFE Shooting Editor for 31 years, he was to hunting and shooting what Babe Ruth was to baseball or what Elvis was to rock and roll.

Jack was the king of gun writers. Every shooter had heard of Jack O'Connor. He was a man so powerful that in a single session at his typewriter, he could sway opinions for or against a particular rifle caliber. Because of Jack's writings, some calibers, such as the .270 and .243, prospered over the years, and others died a quick death.

In 31 years, Jack had written almost 400 columns, in addition to 200 feature stories for OUTDOOR LIFE and more than a dozen hunting and shooting books.

Jack had hunted throughout most of the world and was considered the last word in sheep hunting and rifles. If you had a question about a big-game animal or a gun, you called or wrote to Jack O'Connor. He tried to answer every letter. By his count, he had responded to more than 200,000 pieces of mail.

A few months before the hunt, Jack had called and asked if we could hunt whitetails and pronghorns in Montana. I was overwhelmed at the idea.

I'm a hunter's booking agent. I'd arranged many hunts for Jack in Africa, Canada, Alaska and in the continental United States, and had accompanied him on some of those hunts. But this was the first time I'd have him all to myself because I'd be his guide. I was beside myself with the enormity of it all.

*S*o there we were, sitting on a log in Montana. At least 20 other whitetails were with the big buck, including two other very large bucks that looked like twins but which were easily outclassed by the giant. But Jack was positioned so that he couldn't see the deer.

I knew that the deer wouldn't hang around for very long. In fact, I wondered why they were there at all. The wind was blowing hard, carrying our scent directly to the whitetails. Jack and I were sitting on a log in a fairly open spot, and the deer were milling about in confusion just 50 feet away.

I didn't dare move or talk for fear of spooking the animals. Somehow, I had to call Jack's attention to them. He was sitting on the middle of the log. I was straddling the log so that I could look both ways. Jack was faced one way…the wrong way.

My rifle lay on my lap, along with a five-foot walking stick. Carefully picking up the stick, I eased it around and cautiously poked it into Jack's back, hoping he'd realize that I was trying to signal him.

Because the wind was blowing so hard, Jack jabbed back at the stick, thinking that it was the pesky branch of a willow being shaken by the wind.

The herd of deer eyed us suspiciously. I became totally unnerved. I didn't know what to do. Under other circumstances, I would have shot the buck myself, and that made me even more distressed.

Our hunt was in eastern Montana, the second part of a double-header. Prior to the whitetail hunt, we'd tried for pronghorn antelope in another area.

As it had turned out, the pronghorn hunt had been frustrating and disappointing, though we'd seen some enormous bucks. The only buck taken had been shot by Jack's pal Henry Kaufman, who had accompanied us on both hunts. Also along was my friend Tom Radoumis, whom Jack jokingly nicknamed Zeus because of Tom's Greek ancestry.

I had done some scouting the day before Jack and Henry had arrived, and I had located a very big pronghorn that I judged to have horns between 17 and 18 inches. Another buck, with 16-inch horns, accompanied the larger antelope. Both were phenomenal animals.

My rancher friend had rigged a horse-drawn buckboard from which to hunt. But Jack wasn't feeling well, so we drove the prairie roads in my Suburban.

Both big antelope were where I'd seen them the day before. A third buck, with 15-inch horns, was lying in a draw just below the other two. I had located the trio from a small knoll with my spotting scope, but when I returned to my vehicle with the good news, Jack said that he wasn't up to the walk.

At that point, I realized that Jack O'Connor was failing. My hero seemed old and frail, and I was sad as well as frustrated.

The only chance we had to get close was to drive up a creek bottom on an old homestead road, and then try a short stalk from below. A high ridge separated the road from the bucks, and I figured that we could get reasonably near to the animals.

I was in a hurry, probably driving too fast because I was thinking intently about the huge pronghorns. Suddenly, I looked out the window to my left, and there were the three bucks racing along beside the truck. Before I could react, the bucks veered sharply and dashed onto the road in front of us.

It was just a matter of luck that I didn't run them over. My quick stop jarred all of us, and that was the end of the three pronghorns.

Later in the day, we saw another good buck, but it was not as big as the large pronghorn we'd seen that morning. The animal was standing close to the road.

"Let's try a trick," Jack said. "Drive past the buck until we're out of sight; then, you and Henry get out. Tom and I will park the vehicle where it's visible. That will hold the antelope's attention. Then, you and Henry circle around on foot and shoot.

"I've decoyed lots of sheep that way," Jack continued. "A long time ago, I realized that animals can't count people."

Jack's strategy worked, though at one point in the stalk, I was sure we had blown it. We had crawled past a pond full of geese and had alarmed the birds. They had flushed noisily, and I had expected the buck to take off, but his attention had remained riveted on the vehicle. Henry then made a fine shot, and we had our first pronghorn.

For the next two days, we did a lot of driving, and Tom and I did a lot of walking. Jack was feeling progressively worse, and he complained of being in a lot of pain. I was worried about what would happen if we found a trophy buck and had to make a long stalk.

Despite our efforts. we hadn't located another worthwhile pronghorn close enough for a shot, and just as we were about to give up, I saw a golden eagle land beside a nest on a little rocky knob. The nest seemed to be unusually large, so I climbed the knob to have a look. I knew that the young eagles were fledged and long gone, but I was curious about the bones and remains of the eagle's prey that would litter the immediate vicinity of the nest.

When I reached the knob, I looked down the other side and was startled to see the monster pronghorn bedded down just 100 yards away.

The buck was very distinctive. Not only did he have enormous horns, but he also had very dark cheek patches that almost looked like eyes. I'd never seen an antelope with those markings before. There was no question. It was the same one I'd almost run over with the truck.

I slowly backed away from the knob and ran back to the truck to tell Jack about the antelope. When I reported our great luck, he sat quietly and didn't say anything for a moment. Then, with regret in every word, he spoke.

"I've hunted all my life and never shot a 17-inch antelope," he said. "I'd love to take him, but I don't think that I should climb that hill."

I was shocked and disappointed. "My God," I thought to myself, "Jack isn't going to try for the giant pronghorn!'"

Until this hunt, I had been sure that Jack O'Connor could climb any hill, make any shot, do the impossible. Now, the realization that the dean of American hunters was old hit me hard. It was a helpless feeling.

I didn't press the issue of trying for the antelope. The full realization of Jack's physical condition stopped me. He had been much more aware of his difficulties than I.

"Why don't you go up there and shoot that buck?" Jack said to me. "You've killed two 17-inch antelope. It would be nice to know that a pal of mine is the only man I know of who has taken three."

Shooting a buck meant for Jack O'Connor while Jack sat in the truck was not something I could do. This was his hunt. Either he would shoot the buck or no one would. So we simply returned to the ranch.

$\mathcal{T}$he second ranch, where we hunted whitetails, was in a lovely setting, with old cabins on a bluff above a river bottom surrounded by dense brush, cottonwood trees and lush croplands. Jack was awed at the thought that this area was once home to great herds of bison, elk and large numbers of grizzlies.

I did some scouting the evening before the hunt and saw at least 200 whitetails feeding in the alfalfa and slipping through the dense underbrush. I had seen some huge whitetails on that ranch on previous hunts, and I fully expected Jack to take the biggest buck of his life in the morning.

Guiding America's top gun writer to a giant whitetail would be a highlight in my life. I can remember thinking about where Jack was likely to kill the buck, the kind of shot he would make and how I'd get the buck out. I even envisioned the way the head would be mounted for Jack.

We positioned ourselves in a strategic stand the next morning, waiting for drivers on horseback to push deer around in the brush. It didn't take long for whitetails to show up. Dozens of deer moved by us, including a number of bucks, but none were exceptional. As we watched, it became obvious that Jack was having problems with his vision. He saw few of the deer; and those he saw were fairly close and easily visible.

I'd never seen more whitetails on a drive in my life. They came by constantly, along with foxes, coyotes, raccoons and pheasants. It was a great show. Jack seemed to be enjoying it immensely. We talked of many things.

At one point, he reminisced about driving tigers in India and how often the beaters were mauled by tigers. He noted that if we had been hunting tigers, the situation would have been vastly different for the men on horseback. It was common, Jack said, for tigers to attack elephants and their riders beating the brush.

The subject turned to Jack's hunting preferences.

"What do you like to hunt most?" I asked.

"Sometimes, I think I like to hunt tigers, sometimes sheep, and right now, whitetail deer. I guess that I like to hunt everything, as long as the animal has a fair chance."

After several more drives, the day ended without Jack having fired a shot. But he'd had chances at several respectable bucks. Jack had not wanted to shoot an average buck because he'd taken many such bucks. He had wanted something more.

"I'd like to take one really good whitetail buck," Jack said as we walked to the vehicle. "'But if a hunter wants to shoot big bucks, he must learn not to shoot the small ones. This may mean you go home empty-handed a few times, but that is the difference between hunting and trophy hunting.'"

"It doesn't hurt to be lucky, too," I remarked.

"And maybe 30 years younger," Jack said, as we headed for my truck.

Before we reached the truck, I pointed to a stand high in a tree and told Jack that a hunter had fallen out of the stand and had been killed the previous year.

"I cannot think of a better way to go," Jack said with a slight smile. "I don't want a long, lingering death; I want to die quickly. I'd like to die while on a hunting trip and have my ashes spread over the sheep country in the Yukon."

Jack's words seemed to reinforce a strange feeling I had that this would be his last hunt. Somehow, I believe that he felt it as well.

The next day, while we were driving to a stand, a very large buck ran across the dirt road in front of us. It stopped and looked back. The deer was so close that I could see his bulging eyes.

Instead of running off immediately, the deer stared at us. Jack had difficulty seeing it, and he made a hasty effort to get out of the vehicle. But Jack's bulky winter clothes and boots hung up on the truck door handle and the seat. He cursed his 75 years, the manufacturers of bulky clothes, Stetson hats and long-barreled rifles.

By the time he finally got out, the buck had seen enough and was running through the brush. Although a shot would have been possible, Jack got back in the car and sat without saying a word.

It was obvious that Jack was terribly frustrated and in a great deal of pain from his arthritis. I felt bad for him. In earlier years, no running buck was a match for Jack O'Connor's incredible shooting.

Finally, Jack started to laugh at the humor of the situation.

"I don't think that deer deserved to be shot," he said, grinning. "Anyone who is so old and decrepit that he can't get out of a vehicle while a deer waits to be killed, shouldn't have a shot anyway."

The old hunter had a wry sense of humor, and didn't mind poking fun at himself. But he was frustrated, and we all felt his helplessness.

Later that morning, several whitetails appeared before our stand. Some were very fine bucks. Tom and the horseback riders were doing their best to keep deer in front of us. Occasionally, Jack would raise his rifle, look through the scope, and lower it again. When one particularly good buck went by and Jack didn't shoot, I asked him why he was hesitating.

"I can't see the antlers very well," he said.

Just then, a big buck appeared and stood against a red riverbank.

The buck was a reddish color, and it was standing in the open. I pointed the buck out to Jack, but he couldn't see it. I realized that the only way Jack would be able to see a buck well enough to shoot was if it was in front of a sharply contrasting background. And it would have to be very close.

Despite bad luck throughout both hunts, Jack kept his good humor and told us more stories of his hunts. I think he perceived my personal frustration that he hadn't scored. He was trying to make me feel better. But Tom and I hadn't given up. We were determined to give Jack the best hunt he ever had, with or without luck.

Our next plan was to go to a spot where I'd previously seen a truly big buck. Whitetails normally hang out in the same area, and we hoped to see this particular buck again.

*J*ack and I walked to the log I'd selected to watch from, and now understanding his visual problem, I positioned him where he could look down a narrow corridor that had a light background of grass. A heavy frost as bright as snow provided a contrasting backdrop.

Tom and the other drivers were good. Before long, a number of deer ran in front of Jack and me. A dozen does passed through the corridor Jack was watching. Following was a nice buck that bounded through so fast that Jack couldn't react in time.

More deer, including several good bucks, ran through, and Jack looked at me with a pained expression. "I'm rattled," he said. "I must be coming down with buck fever."

I couldn't believe the deer that were running by. I'd never seen more whitetails in my life. I don't think that Jack was really suffering from buck fever. He was having difficulty seeing antlers, and his old painful limbs simply prevented him from reacting quickly with his rifle.

The wind had begun to blow furiously just before the 210-plus deer, including the giant buck and his twin accomplices mentioned at the beginning, showed up. I firmly believed that the gods were setting the stage for Jack O'Connor's final act.

I'd never been in quite such a predicament before. I was poking Jack in the back. He was jabbing at the stick. And a record-class whitetail was watching our performance.

Instantly, the first two bucks were alarmed by our movements and ran. They made so much noise that Jack quickly turned and saw them disappear into the brush.

"Damn!," he said. "How can my luck be so bad?"

As soon as he spoke, he spotted the big buck, but it was too late. The animal quickly melted back into the willows.

Suddenly, I saw the twin bucks heading back toward the corridor that Jack had been watching. One of them stopped near a dead snag and stared at us.

"'Shoot, shoot," I whispered. But Jack didn't shoot because most of the deer's body was hidden.

"Get ready," I warned. "Here comes the second buck."

I felt foolish telling Jack O'Connor to get ready. He was one of the most knowledgeable hunters I'd ever met, and he was indeed ready, but this was not a good day for Jack. It was like a bad dream. To me, the champion of hunters was now in the ring, under the spotlight, with the crowd cheering. But suddenly, that dream was shattered as the young champion I remembered became the old hunter.

At that moment, I felt a warm but sad kinship with Jack. It was like discovering that your Dad had grown old before your eyes and being stunned by his inability to do the things that both of you had once done so easily. It was like pleading, "Come on, Dad, let's do it," and Dad replying, "I just can't do that anymore, Son."

The two bucks moved away, but they were positioned where I could make a quick dash and possibly force them through the opening where Jack could see them.

I ran, and everything seemed to be going well, but the bucks suddenly vanished, as happens so often with whitetails. They were gone. No amount of wishing could bring them back.

At that moment, the wind stopped and the woods grew silent. I was never so disappointed in my life. I turned around to pick up my rifle, and was astonished to see the giant buck once again. The great whitetail was in the open, standing broadside, looking directly at me.

Picking up my rifle, I slowly turned my head and saw Jack looking the opposite way. He was still watching for the twin bucks that had made off in another direction.

I whispered loudly to signal Jack, but my voice spooked the buck. He whirled and crashed into the willows, bounding off in a way I knew was for keeps.

I was heartsick. Why did so many bucks present themselves, and why were we so unlucky?

Then, the impossible happened. The huge buck stopped running and trotted right back to the very place he had just left. It was too much. I raised my rifle, aimed at his heart, but could not pull the trigger. I was staring at what might have been the biggest buck in Montana, but I couldn't shoot. I desperately longed to hear the roar of Jack's .270. There was no reason in the world why that buck should have

returned and presented himself for another shot. It was as if the good Lord was giving Jack O'Connor the finest show of his life.

I raised my rifle again, but could not bring myself to fire it. This was Jack's hunt, not mine, even though he had insisted that I shoot if I had an opportunity.

The enormous buck spun and ran off, this time for good. I turned and was shocked to see Jack standing with his rifle to his shoulder, aiming at the buck. He was grinning from ear to ear, and I realized that he had seen the buck, but for some reason had refused to shoot.

"God, what a buck," he said simply. "What a buck!"

As we left the woods, our hunt over, I couldn't bring myself to ask Jack why he hadn't shot. Perhaps he'd seen me drawing a bead on the buck and wanted me to take it.

Perhaps. Or maybe he hadn't fired because he believed that once you take the biggest buck of your life, there's nothing to look forward to.

Jack O'Connor passed away the next spring, in 1978. I have returned to the whitetail ranch several times since Jack's death. I never saw the giant buck again, nor have I ever again seen the unbelievable number of bucks that we saw on his last hunt.

I'm convinced that someone up high was pulling for old Jack. Jack was one of the finest hunters and shooting writers who ever lived. It was fitting that he was shown such a superb parade of whitetail bucks the last time he carried a rifle in his beloved American West. ◆

From Outdoor Life, *March 1988*

Photo Credits

Photographers

Charles J. Alsheimer
Bath, NY

© Charles J. Alsheimer: pp. 5, 6, 14-15, 30, 39 all, 42-43 ,58, 80, 112-113, 124, 130, 138, 152

Erwin A. Bauer
Sequim, WA

© Erwin A. Bauer: p. 186

Gary Clancy
Byron, MN

© Gary Clancy: p. 120

Byron Dalrymple
Kerrville, TX

© Byron Dalrymple: p. 202

Charles Elliott
Covington, GA

© Charles Elliott: p. 174

Michael H. Francis
Billings, MT

© Michael H. Francis: p. 73

Donald M. Jones
Troy, MT

© Donald M. Jones: pp. 34-35, 66, 104

Bill Kinney
Ridgeland, WI

© Bill Kinney: pp. 87, 150 both

Lance Krueger
Mc Allen, TX

© Lance Krueger: pp. 23, 50, 147, 149

Bill Marchel
Fort Ripley, MN

© Bill Marchel: pp. 146, 151

Bill McRae
Choteau, MT

© Bill McRae: back cover

Jack O'Connor

© Jack O'Connor: p. 167

David Sams/Texas Inprint
Dallas, TX

© David Sams/Texas Inprint: p. 158

Mark E. Scott
Barrie, VT

© Mark E. Scott: p. 128

Jim Zumbo
Cody, WY

© Jim Zumbo: p. 172

Illustrators

Tom Beecham

© Tom Beecham: p. 193

John Dyess
Glendale, MO

© John Dyess: pp. 24-25, 74, 76, 78

Ken Laager
Lititz, PA

© Ken Laager: pp. 212-213

Charles E. Pearson

© Charles E. Pearson: pp. 97, 100, 102, 103

Leon Parson
Rexburg, ID

© Leon Parson: cover

Jeffrey Terreson
Pound Ridge, NY

© Jeffrey Terreson: p. 127 both